Chrismons

Christian Year Series

INSTRUCTIONS FOR MAKING THE CHRISTIAN YEAR SERIES OF CHRISMONS:

Interpretation, Uses, Patterns, Diagrams, Step-by-Step Directions
for the Chrismons & the Framework; Alternative Plans.
(Formerly the Liturgical Year Series)

by
Frances Kipps Spencer

Ascension Lutheran Church
Danville, VA

CREDITS

PHOTOGRAPHS:
Richard H. Craigue

PUBLICATION:
Kit W. Barkhouser
Gail K. Bengston
Gary L. Bengston
Roy B. Burnett, Jr.
Mary Lee E. Gravely
Robert F. Holley
Judy E. Johnson
Undine H. Kipps
Lucille B. McCoy
Encie A. Napier
Robert V. Shaver
Harry W. Spencer
Jean K. Stahl
Kim M. Stahl
Ruth G. Taylor

"CHRISMONS™" is a Trademark of Ascension Lutheran Church and is protected by the laws of the United States Trademark office. The patterns books are copyrighted and protected by the laws of the United States Copyright office. No part of this publication may be reproduced by any means, without the written permission of the publisher.

Scripture quotations, unless otherwise noted in the text, are from the Revised Standard Version of the Bible, copyright 1946 and 1952 by the Division of Christian Education of the National Council of Churches.

Frances K. Spencer, originator of Chrismons Ornaments, has given all rights to The Lutheran Church of the Ascension, Danville, Virginia. This Church owns the Trademark and the Copyrights.

CHRISMONS: CHRISTIAN YEAR SERIES
Fourth Edition, Revised
Copyright© 2017 by Ascension Lutheran Church,
Danville, Virginia, All Rights Reserved.

Previous Editions
Copyright 1961, 1965, 1972

Published by Ascension Lutheran Church
314 West Main Street, Danville, Virginia 24541, U.S.A.

Eighth Printing

ISBN 0-9715472-1-1

www.chrismon.org · chrismonsministry@gmail.com · facebook.com/ChrismonsMinistry · pinterest.com/Chrismons

CONTENTS

	KEY & SCALE DRAWING	1
	PREFACE	2
I	MEANING OF THE CHRISTIAN YEAR SERIES	3
	Program (Meaning)	3
	References	6
	Notes on the Interpretation	7
	Uses of the Christian Year Series	7
	Terms, Construction Methods	9
II	FRAMEWORK: UNIFYING ELEMENT OF THE SERIES	9
	Selection of Size & Framework Type	9
	Framework to Tree Proportions	10
	Preparations for Making Rigid Frameworks	12
	Construction of Original Rigid Framework	15
	Construction of Simplified Rigid Framework	19
	Hanging Rigid Frameworks on Trees	21
	Flexible Connections: Construction & Hanging	23
III	SEASON & PERSON BORDERS: PATTERNS & DIRECTIONS	24
	Original Glass Bead Circles	24
	Simplified Circles	26
	Present Woven Metal Bead Circles & Squares	26
IV	SEASON & PERSON SYMBOLS: PATTERNS & DIRECTIONS	30
	Selection of Construction Methods	30
	General Directions for Styrofoam Symbols	33
	Rayed Nimbus	33
	Five-Point Star (Epiphany)	34
	Shamrock in Triangle with Circle (Trinity)	35
	Descending Dove (God the Spirit)	36
	Hand from Cloud (God the Father)	37
	Lamb with Banner of Victory (God the Son)	39
	Phoenix Rising from the Flames (Easter)	40
	Pelican-in-Her-Piety (Lent)	43
	Gladiolus, Rose, Lily	46
	Butterfly (Easter)	47
	Scroll with Prophecy (Advent)	49
	Seven-Tongued Flame (Pentecost)	51
	Fiery Chariot (Ascension)	53
V	CROSSES, STARS, & ACCESSORIES	56
	General Directions for Stars	56
	Shell on Eight-Point Star	56
	Chalice on Six-Point Star	56
	Book on Seven-Point Star	57
	Crosses (Full & Half-Size)	59
	Vine Accessories (Tendrils, Leaves, Grapes)	61
	Trinity Cycle Accessories (Pearls, Censers)	62
	OTHER CHRISMON BOOKS AVAILABLE	64
	BENEDICTION	65

Copyright 2016 Jessamyn Rubio Photography

FIGURE 1

Christian Year Series

Key to the symbols and their placement.
(Scale Drawing)
(1" to 1')

Note final finished height is 8 feet. Scale of this page may be off due to digital reproduction. Adjust your project accordingly.

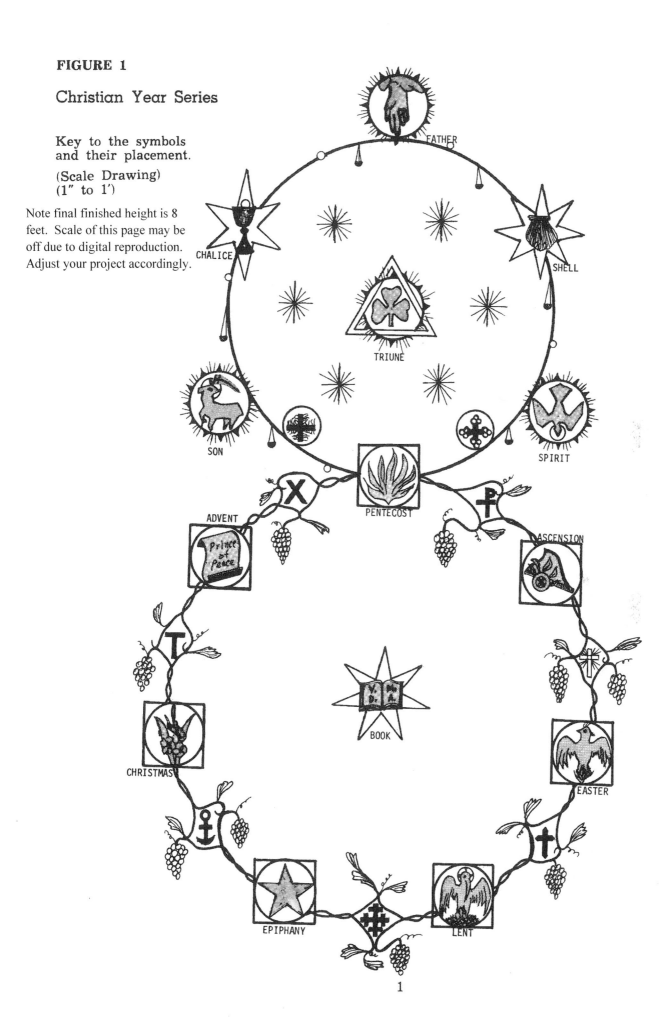

PREFACE

On Christmas Day in the year that was celebrated as the 1959th after the Nativity of our Lord, a lone and lonely visitor to the Chrismon tree in Ascension Church asked the question, "Who is God?"' Consciously and conscientiously, an answer to his question was attempted. But there was no evidence that the words or thoughts reached him. Although the search for him went on for months, he was never found again.

Regret for the apparent failure stayed as accustomed day by day activities followed. One of those activities was studying Christian symbolism so that there would be new Chrismons for the tree the next Christmas. That year, 1960, more time than usual was spent on research. But it was not until a review of what had been learned and accomplished after four months of work that the truth revealed itself. The unconscious longings and conscious efforts had converged on answering that question, "Who is God?"

"Who is God?" "What is He?" "What does He do?" "What has He done?" The Christian Year Series (added to the Chrismon tree in The Lutheran Church of the Ascension in 1960 and formerly called the Liturgical Year Series) answers these questions symbolically. Within the framework of the Church Year, these Chrismons explain, as pictures can, Who and What God is. The Series depicts the Holy Triune and the Life through which God has made the clearest revelation of Himself, the Life through Which He calls and enables all mankind to come to Himself.

* * *

The following interpretation of the Christian Year Series is approximately what was given in The Lutheran Church of the Ascension in 1960. The word "approximately" is used because different people presented the explanation extemporaneously to various groups. Naturally, the talk was adapted to suit the age and background of the listeners. Furthermore, no two people can give exactly the same witness.

While this interpretation summarizes the one that was originally intended, it is not the only correct one. Even though there may be only one accurate historical explanation of a symbol, the meaning of the symbol varies in actual usage with the personal background of the user and the viewer. A few years ago, one may have said that a certain interpretation was incorrect. But time and experience have led to a different opinion. Real symbolism is not shorthand.

Study the historical meanings of the symbols; read and ponder the scriptures; review the drawing of the Series. Then, in prayer and under God's discipline, come to an understanding of what these designs say and mean to you. That is your witness and the only one that you are qualified to give.

Your words may be the same as the ones on the following pages. You may wish to change small parts of the narrative or all of it. Perhaps you will use the Series for some entirely different purpose such as a vehicle for presenting the Apostles' or Nicene Creed. If your interpretation is based on God's Word, if it is rooted in the Life of our Lord, it will be true.

FIGURE 3

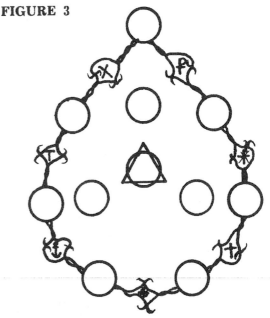

Life Cycle of the Christian Year Series
Trinity & Person symbols at the Center.

Scale: ½" to 1'.

FIGURE 2

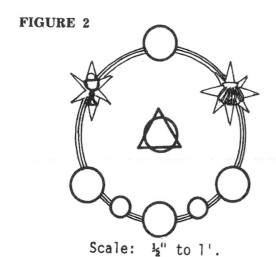

Scale: ½" to 1'.

INTERPRETATION OF THE CHRISTIAN YEAR SERIES

(PROGRAM)

In the beginning, God was. He created heaven and earth, and earth was a paradise. Afterwards, He created man in His own image and set him in this paradise. God and man walked together.

Then man decided that he preferred his own way to God's will, and man disobeyed God. By this sin, man separated himself from his Creator. The earth became a wilderness, and man was lost in the barren desert of his own sin.

Though man had turned his back on his Maker, God still loved him. The Father looked down on His people and had compassion on them. Out of His love, God designed a plan to establish a new fellowship with man. This is the story of that plan as the church lives it annually in her observance of the Christian Year.

* * *

The story begins with the golden scroll of prophecy which symbolizes the promises of salvation which God gave His people. In Advent, the first season of the Christian Year, Christians recall the Old Testament prophecies which foretold the first coming of our Savior. We also remember the New Testament assurances that He will return in all His glory. During this season, we prepare ourselves to receive Him anew. We think of His glory as Isaiah describes it:

"His name will be called 'Wonderful Counselor, Mighty God, Everlasting Father, Prince of Peace.' "[1]

God promised us His Son so that we could walk with Him again as His children. The cross was to be the means by which this promise would become reality for each of us.[2] In Advent, the Child is not yet born; the prohecies are not yet fulfilled. So the cross that is used for this season is the Anticipatory or Old Testament or Tau Cross. Because it is like the cross on which many believe our Lord died except that the upper part is missing, it may be called the incomplete cross. Man's salvation is not yet accomplished.

* * *

In the fullness of time, "the Word became flesh and dwelt among us, and we beheld his glory." A gladiolus symbolizes the Incarnation, the Word made flesh. The word gladiolus is from the Latin word *gladius,* which means sword. A person who uses a sword is called a gladiator. (Both words, gladiator and gladiolus come from the same source.) A glance at the leaves of the plant called the gladiolus shows why. Each leaf looks like a two-edged sword. Thus, the flower is called a gladiolus because it is a sword in plant form, or a LIVING sword.[3]

A study of some of the New Testament letters reveals why the gladiolus has come to symbolize the Incarnation. In the Epistle to the Hebrews, the writer says, "For the word of God is living and active, sharper than any two-edged sword . . ." And who was this Child whose birth is celebrated here? St. John describes Him as the Word made flesh—or the LIVING word—the same LIVING word which is sharper than any two-edged sword. Thus the LIVING sword in plant form symbolizes the LIVING God in human form. It is His birth as a living human being that is the Christmas celebration. The God Who created all and established all natural laws made Himself subject to those laws for us all. This is why the angels sang that night. This is the glory of Christmas.

(Or: Another of Isaiah's prophecies was that one day "the desert would blossom as the rose."[4] In the fullness of time, this prophecy was fulfilled when a virgin conceived and bore a son and called His Name Jesus. The Rose of Love blossomed in the desert of sin that was the world! The promised Messiah was born to set men free from sin! Angels sang that night, and since that time, men who know the Rose of Love sing to God's glory as they celebrate the birth of the Child Who was the Son of God.)

But the shadow of the cross falls over even the birth of the Child; for He was born to die. However, the shadow is not wholly dark because it brings the light of hope. The anchor cross was called the Cross of Hope by Christians of the first century.[5] It is one of the oldest symbols of our faith. It is particularly appropriate for the Christmas season because this Child is the Hope of the world.

There is another interpretation that is especially felicitous at this time of the year. In the anchor, two figures are apparent—the cross and the crescent moon. The cross, a sign for our Savior, rises out of the moon, an ancient symbol for the virgin mother of our Lord.[6]

* * *

Later, wise men who had followed a star came to see the Baby. When His mother showed her Son to them, the men fell down and worshipped Him, for they saw His Glory.[7] During the Epiphany season, the church recalls the ways in which the Child and later the Man was shown to be the Son of God. Christians also remember that the wise men were of another race and land, and they recognize that the Son of Man is the Savior-God not only of the Jews but of all people. The five-point star or Epiphany Star, which the wise men followed, symbolizes this whole season.

It is said that people with imagination can see a person in the five-point star. The top ray is the head; the two points at the sides, the arms; and the bottom ones, the legs.

MEANING

Throughout Epiphany-tide, the church underlines her belief that our Lord is the God of all men by emphasizing missions.8 The cross crosslet reflects this belief. From the central cross, which represents the one on which our Lord died, four crosses grow outward to the four directions of the compass—North, East, South, and West. Thus the true Christian, as he takes up his cross to follow Him, accepts his responsibility to carry the gospel to the four corners of the world, to all people.9

* * *

After our Lord's ministry in Galilee and Judea, He went up to Jerusalem to accomplish that for which He was sent. He carried His cross to Calvary; He died there so that we might live. He was the perfect Sacrifice for our sins.10

Long ago, people believed that in times of famine, a mother pelican would pierce her breast so that her young could drink her life's blood and live.11 Such is a measure of God's love for us. He gave His Son to die so that we could live.12 For many centuries, the pelican-in-her-piety has been a symbol of the Atonement our Savior made for us.

The pelican giving her blood for her young also suggests the Lord's Supper which He instituted on the night before He died. St. Matthew reported His words: "This is my blood which is shed for many for the remission of sins."13

The pelican is different from any other Chrismon on the tree. On this ornament only, we have used a color other than white or gold. The drops of blood on the breast are red.

The pointed ends of the Passion Cross or Cross of Suffering remind us of our Lord's sufferings—of the points of the thorns, the points of the nails, and the point of the spear through His lifeless body. And they laid Him in the tomb . . .14

* * *

But three days later, He burst forth from the tomb.15 Like the glory of the rising sun, He conquered death. The shameful cross, out of suffering and death, became a thing of glory. On Easter morning, we see the cross as the Cross in Glory—an ordinary Latin cross—but illumined by the rays of a rising sun. Our Lord, the Son of righteousness is risen and lives now and forever.16

The phoenix symbolized resurrection long before the era when Jesus of Nazareth lived. It was a legendary bird of great beauty that lived, ancient Egyptians believed, in the Arabian desert. When this bird reached an age of about five hundred years, it constructed a funeral pyre on which it threw itself. After the fire died down, a small worm appeared in the ashes. In three days, the worm grew to again become a phoenix, more beautiful than ever, to live another five hundred years.

It is not surprising, in view of the three days that the Man called Jesus spent in the tomb, that, by the third century, Christians used the phoenix as a symbol for their Lord's resurrection. Christian symbolism is derived from many sources—as many sources as there are influences in the backgrounds of the individual Christians. A study of these symbols is a study of the whole culture of all peoples who call the Christ their King.

(Or: Nothing seems more dead than the drab mass into which the larva goes to rest during its pupa stage. But suddenly, from the lifeless chrysalis, there emerges a beautiful butterfly! One can't believe it is happening! But there it is in full view! A radiantly beautiful new creature! This must have been something of the feeling of our Lord's disciples when they began to be aware that He lived again. The life cycle of the butterfly suggests something of the unexpected joy and the incredibly altered lives of those who knew that the Lord had conquered death.)

* * *

Outside of our Lord Himself, the Jewish writings of the Old Testament exerted the greatest influence on the Son of Man's first disciples. The use of Elijah's fiery chariot as a symbol for our Lord's Ascension illustrates this point.17 In drawing a parallel between certain events which are described in the Old Testament with episodes in the Life of our Lord, the early church followed her Savior's example. One recalls the time when the Christ explained, "Even as Moses lifted up the serpent in the wilderness, so must the Son of Man be lifted up."18

The Old Testament event which is used to illustrate some action in the perfect Life is called a "type." Since Elijah was caught up to Heaven bodily in a fiery chariot, a picture of the chariot is used to depict our Savior's bodily Ascension into Heaven.19 There He sits in glory on the right hand of His Father.

The triumph of the ascended Son of God is reflected in the form of the Chi Rho which is called the Cross of Constantine. Most people have heard the legend of how Constantine became the first Roman emperor to embrace Christianity. During a definitive battle for the city of Rome, he saw a sign in the sky with the words, "In this sign conquer." Whether the sign that he was reputed to have seen was the cross or the Greek abbreviation for Christ, the Chi Rho, is unknown. But it is certain that, after that military campaign was successfully concluded, he placed the Chi Rho symbol on his labarum or imperial standard. Thus, the Chi Rho became associated with triumph. In addition to the original Greek meaning, a Latin (Constantine's language) interpretation was given to the letters—*Christus Rex* or Christ, the King.20

On Ascension Day, Christians around the world celebrate the completion of their Lord's earthly Life and His triumphant return to His glory with His Father in Heaven. This divine victory is illustrated with a cross that is associated with the earthly triumph of His body the church when Constantine, the ruler of the known world of that era, became a Christian and his empire with him.

* * *

Before the Man Who was called Jesus left His disciples, He told them that His Father would send the Counselor.[21] When they were gathered together on the Pentecost after His Ascension, the Holy Spirit came upon our Lord's apostles like tongues of flame.[22] The church, the body of Christ on earth, came into being. From that day until now, the church has presented the living Christ to all the world. Until her Lord returns to claim His kingdom, the church will continue to make His Name known. The seven-tongued flame symbolizes the outpouring of the gifts of the Holy Spirit on Pentecost.[23]

A flaming cross, the Cross Flamant, depicts the fiery zeal which fills every Christian who has been inspired by that same Spirit.[24]

The circle of the Life of our Lord has made its full turn. Back at the beginning, it can be remembered that just as the Christ promised that He would send the Comforter, it was through this same Person that our Lord first came to earth. That fact is affirmed in the Nicene Creed, "He was incarnate by the Holy Ghost of the Virgin Mary."[25] And through the power of this same Person, our Lord comes to us too. By the Gift of the Holy Spirit, we have the living Christ with us always.[26]

* * *

The longest season of the Liturgical Year remains. During the season of Trinity, the church worships and glorifies the one living God and studies the teachings of the One by Whom God revealed Himself to man. The whole upper part of this figure depicts the Holy Trinity.

Three devices combine to symbolize the Triune. In the center is the shamrock composed of three leaves on one stem. It is said that an Irish priest, Patrick, first used the shamrock to attempt to explain the inexplicable Nature of one God in three Persons. Although the equilateral triangle is only one geometric figure, it has three separate and distinct sides. It has been used for centuries to suggest the one God Who has presented Himself to man in three different Ways. The endless circle defines the eternal Nature of God Who was before time and Who will be when time is no more.

In each corner of the triangle, there is a smaller shamrock, this time constructed of shells, which symbolizes Holy Baptism. Two of the few references to the three Persons of the Triune in the Gospels have a connection with baptism: When our Lord was baptized, the voice of God the Father came from Heaven saying, "Thou art my beloved Son; with thee I am well pleased," and the Holy Spirit descended on the Christ like a dove.[27] Just before He ascended into heaven, our Savior commanded: "Go therefore and make disciples of all nations, baptizing them in the name of the Father and of the Son and of the Holy Spirit."[28]

On the circle that surrounds the shamrock-triangle-circle design, one sees a symbol that originated in the written Word for each Person of the Godhead. The hand descending from a cloud refers to God the Father Who created all things. Use of the hand to suggest the Father God is common throughout the Bible. It is first found in the book of Exodus.[29]

Isaiah was the first prophet to depict God the Son as the sacrificial Lamb.[30] In our rendering, the Lamb of God bears the banner of victory over sin and the death of the cross. The lamb in various forms has been the most enduring symbol for the second Person of the Holy Trinity.

All four of the Evangelists report how God the Spirit descended, like a dove, on the Man called Jesus when He was baptized.[31] To depict the third Person of the Triune, the descending dove is at the third point of the imaginary triangle on the upper circle of the figure.

Because each arm of the Cross Treflée terminates in three circles, it reminds us that each Person of the Triune, God the Father, God the Son, and God the Spirit, participates in our salvation.

It is impossible to completely explain the Mystery of the Holy Trinity with finite minds. The best that can be done is to say that these are some of the things that are known about God. The Chrismon in the center symbolizes God in His completeness; it is separate from the circle because "no man has seen God."[32] But God has made Himself known to man in three ways: As the Father, as the Son, and as the Holy Spirit. In these revelations, we know that which is sufficient for us.

* * *

The three stars and the censers and pearls that are scattered along the top circle symbolize the ways in which God comes to us. Since Old Testament times, censers, or incense burners, have suggested prayer.[33] The pearls symbolize the Word of God.[34]

Another symbol for the written Word is an open book on the seven-point star. The letters V. D. M. A. stand for the Latin *"Verbum Dei Manet in Aeternum,"* "The Word of God endureth for ever."[35] The seven-point star refers to the Holy Spirit Who inspired the writers of the Word as it appears in the Bible.[23]

The individual receives the gift of the Spirit in Holy Baptism, which is pictured by the shell on the eight-point star.[36] In his first letter, St. Peter inspired the use of any eight part, sided, or pointed figure as symbolic of man's regeneration through Baptism.[37]

MEANING

The chalice and wafer on the six-point star depict the Lord's Supper at which the Son Himself is present. The points of the star recall Isaiah's vision: "The spirit of wisdom and understanding, the spirit of counsel and might, the spirit of knowledge, and the fear of the Lord."38 Together the three stars represent the Means of Grace or the ways in which the one God comes to each person who believes.

* * *

One more cross must be passed before the figure on the tree is complete. While most Chrismons use an X as the letter Chi, the first letter of Christ in Greek, the X shape at this point is St. Andrew's Cross. It is believed that the Apostle Andrew was martyred on a cross of this shape. In its use here, St. Andrew's cross symbolizes the whole church—all the apostles and saints who have believed in and who still accept Christ Jesus as their Lord and Savior.

St. Andrew's Cross is used to depict the whole community of believers because the Church Year begins with the Sunday closest to St. Andrew's Day, November 30th. It was the church, the body of Christ, which developed the pattern of living with our Lord that is called the Liturgical or Christian Year. In addition, it is fitting that a symbol for the "first called" of the Christ's apostles should denote all who have been called.39

* * *

A closer look at the lower loop or cycle, which represents the Life of our Savior, discloses that the major events of the Life of Jesus of Nazareth are linked to each other with a vine. On the vine are grapes, which are the fruit. They remind us of our Lord's description of Himself as related by St. John in the fourteenth chapter of his gospel. The Son of God said, "I am the vine, you are the branches. He who abides in me, and I in him, he it is that bears much fruit."40

* * *

These symbols of the seasons—the gladiolus, the star, the pelican, and the others—refer to historical events that happened in the Life of a Man Who lived many years ago. The vine was a symbol which that Man used to describe Himself to His apostles who lived with Him. But that description was not only for those men who lived in that age. Those words were said to all people of all eras. They are said to you, today. For the Vine still lives!

Today—now—our Lord says to each of you and to me, "I am the vine, and you are the branches. Abide in Me and I in you. It is the man who shares My Life and whose life I share who bears fruit that lasts." The grapes on this vine symbolize that fruit. They symbolize the fruit not only of our Lord's first disciples who walked the earth with His physical Being, but also the fruits of all the saints who lived with Him down through the ages. They symbolize also the fruit that, through His grace and in His love, you may bear to His glory.41

REFERENCES

1) Isaiah 9:6.
2) Numbers 21:9; John 3:14, 15.
3) John 1:1-14; Hebrews 4:12.
   Also see Genesis 3:23, 24.
4) Isaiah 35:1 (King James).
5) Hebrews 6:19; Matthew 12:21; Romans 15:12.
6) Isaiah 7:14; Matthew 1:18-25.
7) Matthew 2:1-11; Revelation 22:16; Numbers 24:17.
8) Matthew 28:19; Acts 1:8.
9) Mark 8:34; Luke 9:23.
10) Hebrews 10:12.
11) Psalms 102:6 (King James); 101:7 (Douay).
12) I Thessalonians 5:9, 10; John 3:16.
13) Matthew 26:27, 28.
14) John 19.
15) I Corinthians 15:3, 4.
16) Malachi 4:2.
17) II Kings 2:11.
18) John 3:14.
19) Acts 1:9-11.
20) I Timothy 6:15.
21) John 14:26.
22) Acts 2:1-4.
23) Revelation 5:12.
24) Romans 12:11.
25) Matthew 1:20.
26) John 14:26.
27) Mark 1:9-11.
28) Matthew 28:19.
29) Exodus 3:19; 15:6; 24:16.
30) Isaiah 53:7; John 1:29; Revelation 5:12; 17:14; 6:16, 17.
31) Matthew 3:16; Mark 1:10; Luke 3:22; John 1:32.
32) John 1:18.
33) Psalms 141:2; Revelation 5:8.
34) Matthew 7:6.
35) Isaiah 40:8; I Peter 1:25 (New English, Douay).
36) Acts 2:38.
37) I Peter 3:20, 21.
38) Isaiah 11:2.
39) John 1:35-42; I Corinthians 12:26; Ephesians 4 & 5; Colossians 1:18.
40) John 15:1-11.
41) Galatians 5:22, 23.

MEANING

NOTES ON THE INTERPRETATION

LENT:

When the Christian Year Series was first placed on the tree at Ascension Lutheran Church, the only Chrismon with any color was the pelican-in-her-piety. But since then, occasional ornaments have been made which have a touch of color either for emphasis or to clarify the meaning. Consequently, the explanation now is: "The pelican is different from most Chrismons on the tree. It is one of the very few ornaments on which a color other than white or gold appears."

CHRISTMAS:

While the rose is the most popular symbol for the Nativity (outside of the manger, of course), the gladiolus, even though it is a rarer figure, points to the most important element of the Christmas season. In the Roman Catholic Church, the rose refers to the Mother of our Lord. By extension, it can symbolize the Nativity. But such usage may be ambiguous.

The origin of the rose symbol is Isaiah 35:1, King James Version. In the Revised Standard Version, however, the crocus becomes the symbol of the Messianic Promise. Other translations add more flowers to the list based on this text. Consider these points as well as the two interpretations before deciding which symbol to use.

EASTER:

Even though there is historical authority (catacombs) for use of the phoenix, some may question its pagan origin. The Easter lily, of recent origin, is ambiguous (the lily is traditionally associated with the Virgin Mary) and has no more to recommend its use than any spring blooming bulb. However, it IS widely known and in the current culture MEANS Easter to the average person more than any other symbol.

The butterfly expresses the explosive quality of the Resurrection much better than the lily and does not have the pagan association of the phoenix. But the church did not use it widely in the past. Further, its life cycle is such an excellent symbol for Christian life (larva—life on earth; chrysalis or pupa—death; butterfly—resurrection in Christ) that some prefer to keep it for that use.

Other Easter symbols seem less adequate. Perhaps someone can think of a new figure. But then, nothing in this world can ever compare to our Lord's Resurrection. For this reason, the emphasis of the Easter interpretation is placed on the Cross in Glory rather than the season symbol.

If the Christian Year Series is made by the simplified method, the group has three styrofoam birds when the phoenix is the Easter symbol. This similarity would tend to weaken the impact of each. So the recommendation is against the use of the phoenix in the simplified Series.

It is possible that the size of the Chrismons will influence the selection of both the Easter and Christmas symbols. A natural rose is too small to be effective on the church size Series. But its proportions are just right for the home size for which the gladiolus is too large. Or, a slightly enlarged Messianic Rose, made by the instructions in *Chrismons for Every Day* under "Wreaths," would fit the church size.

Likewise, Easter lilies would be too large for the home size Series. But the butterfly can be made in any size. Since the smaller designs are generally made in styrofoam, the phoenix should not be used in the reduced size.

BOOK ON SEVEN-POINT STAR:

The abbreviation for the Latin *"Verbum Dei Manet in Aeternum"* is V.D.M.A.; for the English translation of the phrase "the Word of God endureth for ever," W.G.E.F.

HOW TO USE THE CHRISTIAN YEAR SERIES

The Christian Year Series tells the story of our Lord and God within the framework of the Liturgical Year. It consists of fourteen large Chrismons (one for each Person of the Trinity, each season of the Church Year, and each of the Means of Grace), nine crosses, a framework to connect them, and minor accessories. Each symbol in the set has its own historical interpretation. But placing them in the suggested sequence gives the individual symbols additional meanings which point to deeper truths.

Primarily, these Chrismons were designed to be the means by which the tree at Ascension could answer the question, "Who is God?" By using the Series as the theme, members of the Church were able to present the Good News to visitors to the Church during the 1960 Christmas season. But even before the ornaments were completed, it was apparent that they could be considerably more than tree decorations.

The Christian Year Series has proved to be a valuable teaching aid throughout the year. It has been used effectively in classes for adults and children in many churches; it has been the means of interpreting the Liturgical Year to non-liturgical groups of all sizes. In addition, it has provided the subject for newspaper, radio, and TV publicity that has reached many outside as well as those in the church.

Either the parts or the whole Series may be used as a permanent decoration in institutions, churches, and homes. It is an inspirational and instructive hanging for an assembly room, class room, library, study, or parlor. At the Lutheran Theological Southern Seminary in Columbia, South Carolina, the Series hangs in a prominent position at the entrance of the Student Union Building throughout the year.

(Those who have known the Chrismons for some years may notice the change in the name

MEANING

of this group from the Liturgical to the Christian Year Series. Dr. F. Eppling Reinartz, former President of Southern Seminary gave the title, "The Christian Year" to these Chrismons when he first saw them assembled in their proper sequence. Because the name was more apt than the original one, it was adopted.)

* * *

The first year that the Christian Year Series was on Ascension's tree, the Christmas pageant was based on the design. This presentation of the Life of our Lord followed the lower or "Life" cycle of the Series. The tree was on one side of the nave. On the other side was a small stage, about seven by seven feet and two and a half feet high. Curtains, about six feet high, ran diagonally across the stage to cut off the back and hide the sacristy door.

While two speakers, alternating between the lectern and the pulpit, gave the scriptural reference and explanation of the symbol, a spotlight (sealed-beam flashlight) was held on the Chrismon. Then, as the Junior Choir sang a carol which referred to the events depicted, little "angels" pulled back the curtains to show a lighted tableau composed of the youngest children. This simple pageant was meaningful and yet easy to produce.

* * *

When one describes this Series as it hangs on a tree or elsewhere, a flashlight is the best pointer. (A pointer is necessary if the listeners are to follow the speaker.) The candlepower should be strong enough to stand out even when the room is fully lighted. The beam must be concentrated so that it points to only one design at a time and does not confuse the viewer by spreading over several ornaments at once. When the light is held by the speaker, it can be easily moved to any Chrismon regardless of how high that design may be on the tree.

* * *

While the parts of the Christian Year Series were designed to be used together, each symbol can stand alone. It is not necessary to reject the whole Series just because the entire group is not wanted. Use the Trinity or Life cycle alone. Or use any of the designs as individual tree decorations just as the Chrismons that are shown in any of the other books. Feel free to select those ornaments that emphasize the things that you want your tree to say. Add to them, if you wish, to point to a truth that you want to share. God is too big to be contained in the mind of one person or even in one group. It is important that each of us, through God's inspiration, give our own witness.

Many groups make the Christian Year Series over a period of years. Until the whole set is complete, season symbols hang on the tree as separate Chrismons. If there is any chance that these designs will be used as a unit, read the framework directions before any Chrismons are constructed. A little advance planning will insure that the ornaments will be usable when the Series is finally assembled.

* * *

When the Christian Year Series is on the tree, it is not advisable to duplicate it elsewhere in the church's decorations. Likewise, it is not wise to repeat Chrismons in the Series at other places on the tree. Doing either would detract from the Series itself.

DIVIDING THE SERIES:

To achieve formal balance, many congregations have two Christmas trees of equal size, one on either side of the nave or chancel. Repetition of the Christian Year Series on each tree would be too mechanical. There is a natural division of meaning in the Series: The Trinity cycle and the Life cycle. For use on two trees, place the Life cycle in a teardrop shape on one tree and the Trinity cycle in a circle on the other. The meaning of the whole Series remains the same; each tree has its own focal point; and the bulk of decoration is almost evenly divided between the two trees.

In the above division, place the Pentecost symbol atop the Life cycle—"Was incarnate by the Holy Ghost," and "I will send Him (the Counselor) to you." The interpretation of St. Andrew's Cross as it is used in the Series and the meaning of the Cross Flamant are related. Between Advent and Pentecost, use either cross or, preferably, make a fiery St. Andrew's Cross and combine the meanings.

Place the book with the seven-point star on the Trinity circle in place of the Pentecost symbol. The book and star can relate to the Son (the Word incarnate) or the Spirit (Who inspired the written Word). The Cross Treflée may be repeated around the circle between the stars and Person symbols. For variety, alternate the Latin, Greek, and Tau forms of the Cross Treflée.

In churches where the tree is decorated around its circumference, this division allows the Life cycle to appear on one side and the Trinity cycle on the opposite. Page 12 gives the practical directions and measurements for dividing the Series in the above manner.

USING HALF THE SERIES:

The Life cycle in the teardrop shape which is described above may be used alone on one tree. Some churches do not observe Trinity as a season. This is also a way for churches without the height for a full size Series to use the full size Chrismons in this group. There is space to hang the full size Person symbols, centered with the figure for the Triune, inside the teardrop. The stars could become separate Chrismons for the tree. In this case, the interpretation would need only slight alterations. Or place the stars in the teardrop and use the Trinity and Person symbols as individual ornaments.

TERMS; CONSTRUCTION METHODS

The "original" Christian Year Series was placed on the tree in Ascension Church in 1960. Because the Series was so meaningful to those who saw the tree, it was decided to share the instructions for making it. But some of the materials that went into the original Chrismons of the Series were no longer available; certain designs were difficult to execute, and the group was too large for some trees. Consequently, instructions for making these ornaments could have only limited appeal.

The solution was to redesign the Christian Year Series. In January of 1961, work began on a reduced size "simplified" version. After the project was successfully completed, directions were written for both the original and simplified Series; patterns for both the full-size and the half-size designs were included.

Over the years since then, several variations and/or additions have been made in the original set. Some changes increase the durability of the decoration; others add to the meaning or slightly alter it; still more take advantage of new materials that have come on the market since the first set was made. In time, the "present" Series came into being.

* * *

The following pages include the instructions for the original, the simplified, and the present Christian Year Series. One need not be wary of constructing any part of the Series by any of these methods. Each is recommended because each tells the same story. After all, it does not matter whether the lamb is made of fresh water pearls or of styrofoam. Each has the same meaning, and it is the meaning that is vital. Feel free to choose whichever method best meets your needs and talents.

In general, the present methods are recommended because they provide the easiest, most durable, and most effective way of presenting the Christian Year witness. On the other hand, the original method may be preferred when it is less expensive. Those who are primarily interested in the very easiest construction and the lowest possible cost will select the simplified symbols on flexible connections.

One should also remember that the parts of the Series are interchangeable. The original season symbols may be used on the flexible connections; the present symbols can appear on the original framework; or the simplified Chrismons can hang on the present frame. Designs may even be selected from any catagory at will for use as individual tree ornaments. The Chrismon maker should realize that he or she has the utmost latitude in selecting from any of the proffered construction methods.

Notice also that some directions overlap. Instructions for the present Trinity cycle are exactly the same as those for one of the simplified methods. All the Advent symbols are the same except that the half-size design employs fewer words than the full-size ornament.

Before making any final decisions, compare the pictures of the Series in this book. The front cover shows the simplified Series on a simplified framework; the picture on the back depicts the present framework and symbols; the photograph on the credit page (just after the title page) is of the original framework and designs; and page 21 shows the half-size Christian Year designs with flexible connections.

* * *

From this introduction, it is obvious that no one will use all the following instructions. Rather one will select the methods that best suit his or her abilities and requirements and follow the directions that pertain to that procedure only. Reading the instructions and studying the diagrams while remembering one's own resources will help to decide which method to use. This may be done, independently, in each category of construction—in the selection of the framework size and type, in the choice of the individual season and Person symbols, and in the decisions about the accessories

THE FRAMEWORK: Unifying Element of the Series

When Chrismons in the Christian Year Series are placed on a tree as individual ornaments, decisions as to their size and placement are the same as for other decorations. But use of these Chrismons as a set requires that they be connected to each other. The separate ornaments become one large decoration which may be over half as tall as the tree.

If the Church Year Series is properly placed, its individual symbols seem to hang like other decorations on the tree. The only apparent difference is that a vine joins the ornaments to each other. This connection enables viewers to follow the message of the Series easily. In addition, the double loop gives the tree a focal point. To realize this effect, the figure 8 must be in proper proportion to the tree's height. While the double loop dominates other Chrismons on the tree, it must not detract from the outline of the tree as a whole.

To use and show the Christian Year Series most effectively in your particular situation, consider the following points:

1) Individual designs should be large enough so that everyone in the church can identify them.

All the details need not be seen.

2) Placement on the tree should allow the Chrismons to be visible from the majority of seats in the room where the tree is located.

3) Placement of the Series should be high enough so that, even when a church or room is fully occupied, the bottom ornaments may be seen from the back pews or seats.

4) Proper proportions between the sizes of the tree, the Chrismons, and the framework must be maintained for aesthetic satisfaction.

In your own room, you may not be able to realize all these aims. Determine which are most important to you and try to achieve them.

While considering the above goals, remember these factors:

1) The type of framework governs the method of hanging and the placement of the individual Chrismons and, consequently, their size.

2) Separate rigid frameworks can be made for the Life and the Trinity cycles. For two trees, place the Life cycle on one, the Trinity cycle on the other. If a tree is decorated around its circumference, one cycle can hang on one side and the other on the opposite side. Or the Life cycle may be used alone on a short tree. See the second column on page 8.

CONNECTIONS FOR THE SERIES

PRESENT RIGID FRAMEWORK

At Ascension Church, a framework of copper pipe is attached to the tree trunk to hold the Christian Year Series. The frame includes the vine and a place to attach every part of the Series. The back cover shows the whole unit.

Advantages: The exact and regular spacing of the symbols in the Series makes its appearance more forceful and its meaning clearer. Hanging the separate parts of the Series on the tree is simple. Ornaments automatically face the way that they should; a strong point of attachment for every item is at the exact place where it is needed. The framework is sturdy enough to be used year after year and adaptable enough to place on various sizes and types (within limits, of course) of trees. Furthermore, the framework is designed so that that Series can be used as an independent decoration for diversified purposes. It can be attached to a wall from behind, placed on a pole with a weighted base, or suspended from overhead by only a wire.

Disadvantages: Construction of the rigid framework requires more time and skill than the flexible connections. Its use for full-size Chrismons may require a taller tree to maintain proper proportions than will fit the situation.

ORIGINAL RIGID FRAMEWORK

A picture of the original Series on the original framework is on the page after the title page. Advantages and disadvantages of the present rigid framework apply to the original. The only difference between the two is in the construction of the Trinity cycle. On the original, the Person symbols are set into the circle. The present Trinity cycle is one continuous tube from which the symbols extend outward. Thus, the present framework is more durable and easier to make. Since the Person symbols need not be an integral part of the Trinity circle, the framework is as meaningful as the original. While there is a slight shift in emphasis, both designs point to the one God in three Persons.

SIMPLIFIED RIGID FRAMEWORKS

The front cover pictures one of these designs. It has all the advantages of the present framework over the flexible connections and can be made in a third of the time that is needed to build the present. In addition, its full-size height is ten inches less than the original.

The season symbols and crosses are appendages rather than an integral part of the cycle circle. Thus, the meaning and appearance of the Series are not as forceful as the original and present. Because the simplified framework must be made in one piece, storage could be a problem.

RIGID FRAMEWORK FOR THE LIFE CYCLE ONLY

This has the same advantages and disadvantages as other rigid frameworks over flexible connections. But the meaning of the Trinity section is less clear. Still, this rigid framework enables full-size Chrismons to be used on trees as short as thirteen feet. See page 2.

FLEXIBLE CONNECTIONS

The photographs on pages 21 and 22 show some symbols and crosses joined to each other with flexible connections. After the ornaments are hung on the tree to duplicate their pattern on the rigid framework as nearly as possible, the connections are hooked from one symbol to the next in the sequence.

Advantages: Construction of the vine is within the abilities of anyone who can make the Chrismons. Full-size Chrismons can be used even if the tree is only twelve feet tall.

Disadvantages: Hanging the Series by this method is difficult. Regardless of how hard one tries, it is impossible to duplicate the regular spacing of the Series on a rigid framework. Thus, the total effect of the Series is weaker, and the sequence and relationships of the parts are not as easy to follow.

FRAMEWORK TO TREE PROPORTIONS

Pages 11 and 12 show diagrams of trees which are decorated with various framework types. Study the diagrams to determine the size and type of framework most suitable in your situation. In your consideration, remember that,

FRAMEWORK

while patterns are given for full and half-size Chrismons, the larger ones are designed to accompany the church-size ornaments in other Chrismon books. Also note the visibility of the half-size crosses. They are recognizable for only about thirty-five or forty feet.

FIGURE 4: PRESENT & ORIGINAL FRAMEWORKS:

The first two illustrations at the right show the figure 8 made by the directions with no variation in shape or scale.

Depending on the species, the tree's top four or five feet is too narrow or thin to provide a proper background for the full-size Trinity circle. If the tree is very wide, the framework may be higher. Construction at the top of the present framework allows it to be placed six inches higher than the original. So, six inches may be subtracted from the top figures for the present full-size diagrams. Deduct proportionate amounts from the part-size figures.

For everyone in the church to see the entire figure, its lowest point should be at least six feet above the floor when the tree stands on the same level as the people who are viewing it. Five feet above the floor is enough when viewers are seated; four feet is too close. Four feet is called ideal for the half-size Series only because visibility for this size is so much less that one need not be too concerned about heads getting in the way.

Apparent proportions of a tree often differ from its real size. If a tree is in a corner of a nave, pews block off the view of the lowest 2½ feet of the tree from any point in the room. Thus, the bottom 2½ feet do not exist for visual effects. The figures take this hidden 2½ feet into account. If the tree is raised so that it can be seen to its base, the Series may be three feet closer to the bottom of the tree.

While the "satisfactory" proportions are not as good as the "ideal," they are workable. For some trees they may be better. The shape of a tree varies with its species. Consider your own tree's shape in making your plans. Ascension Church uses a cedar which is thinner in relationship to its height than most evergreens.

FIGURE 5: SIMPLIFIED RIGID FRAMEWORK:

The full-size simplified framework is only eight feet tall. In addition, its construction allows it to be six inches higher on the tree than than the original framework.

FIGURE 6: ALTERED RIGID FRAMEWORK:

By altering the shape of the double loop as shown opposite, the rigid framework may be used on a shorter tree. This adaptation works when the tree is wide in proportion to its height. If a tree is slim, the framework must be wrapped around the tree. If too much curve is in the framework, the entire Series is not visible from one location.

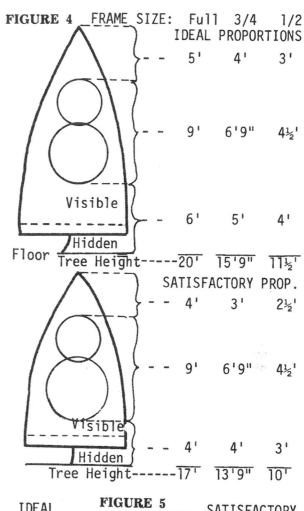

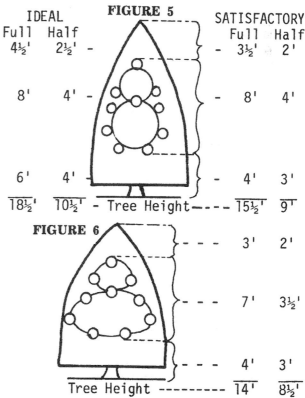

FIGURE 7

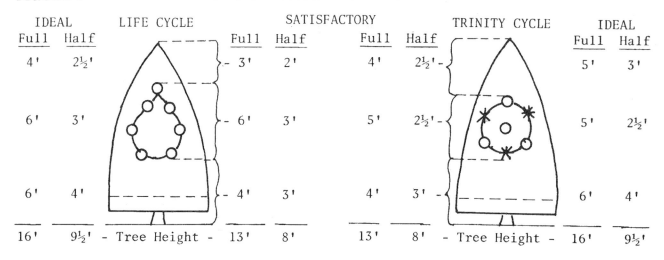

SERIES DIVIDED FOR TWO TREES

PREPARATIONS FOR MAKING A RIGID FRAMEWORK

TALENTS & ABILITIES

Abilities needed to construct the rigid frameworks are somewhat different from those used to make individual Chrismons. In most groups, different people do the two jobs. But since there is a matter of fitting the one to the other, coordination between the two should be good.

If an artist who does wire or metal sculpting is available, just turn the construction of the rigid framework over to him. He will not only do the job but he will probably figure out better methods than are suggested here. If your group is not that fortunate (most are not), here is what is needed: Someone with artistic talent to draw the pattern, understand and interpret the instructions, supervise the construction, and coordinate the work with the Chrismon makers; someone with the know-how and skill to work copper tubing. The same person can do both jobs, but one does not generally find him ready-made.

Any person with a little artistic sense who is willing to adapt to new media can do the first job. The most likely candidates for the second are: An electrician or telephone linesman used to working heavy wires or a plumber IF they are willing to try to do things that they have never attempted before; or a willing-to-learn-do-it-yourselfer. Actually, the above occupational skills are not needed. Ascension Church used a do-it-yourself artist, an architect, and a radio engineer. Many groups have made the framework with no more than willing do-it-yourselfers. But these are the fields in which to search for ready-made skills. The main requirement is the courage to try to do something new.

If more than one person works on the frame, each should read all the framework instructions whether they pertain to his job or not. Each must understand the others' problems. The main task is to construct a vine. Since a vine is a living thing, irregularities are a part of it. But those irregularities must be natural. Artistic sense is needed to know where to allow freedom of expression. At the same time, the framework has a certain weight to support from a fixed point of balance. The materials which are used have definite limitations. The finished product must exactly fit items made by others. Consequently, artistic freedom must be tempered by what is practical and workable.

Here is a safety check: We will not tell you where to get the materials for the framework nor anything more about how to work them than is given in the following directions. We do not mean to withhold needed help. But if your workers do not know these things or how to find out about them in normal channels (the materials and methods of working them are common knowledge in their field), you do not have people with the necessary drive to make the rigid framework. Enough explanations! It is time to work!

PATTERNS

The sketch of the Christian Year Series on page 1 is (except for the ornaments on it) a drawing of the present full-size framework on the scale of one inch to one foot. For the half-size framework, the scale would be one inch to six inches. Figure 21 on page 19 is a drawing, on the same scale, of the simplified rigid framework. A comparison of this drawing with the picture of the simplified Series on the front cover shows that the season circles can lie either inside or outside the Life cycle. Since the only difference between the present and the original framework is in the Trinity cycle, the original Trinity cycle only is diagrammed on Figure 2 on page 2. Note that the scale on that picture is one-half inch to one foot. Combine that Trinity cycle with the Life cycle of the present diagram for the complete original pattern.

FRAMEWORK

Figure 3 on page 2 is a diagram of the teardrop Life cycle on the scale of one-half inch to one foot. Follow this pattern for the use of the Life cycle alone or for the division of the Series for two trees. In the latter case, use either the present or original drawing for the Trinity cycle except, to more closely approximate the teardrop's size, increase the Trinity circle to 3½ feet if the present is used or to four feet if the original is the pattern.

MATERIALS

The framework is constructed of pieces of shaped copper pipe which are soldered into sections. The present (and the original) framework is in seven sections: The Trinity cycle, which includes the Pentecost circle, and six vine sections. It is easy to move the pieces and bolt them together at the place of use. If storage and transportation are no problem, make the present or original framework stronger by constructing it in one piece. The simplified framework must be made in one piece. The Life cycle alone may be built either in one or in seven sections; the Trinity circle must be made in one piece.

For the full-size framework, use flexible or soft drawn copper tubing in two sizes: 3/8" ID and 1/4" OD. If the half-size framework is made, use 1/4" OD pipe throughout. Since the three-quarter size is borderline, make your own selection of tube size.

Cut pieces of pipe are shaped by hand on a jig, and/or twisted with tools to the outline of your actual size pattern. Then, they are soldered together (sometimes after bolting) to form the sections. Each sweated or soldered joint is filed smooth. Holes are drilled and/or screws are attached to make places on or at which to attach the parts of the Series. Finally, the whole framework is spray-painted gold.

TOOLS

Tools that are needed are the ordinary ones used to do the above work. Only one may be difficult to obtain — two heavy cable twisters, which are used by linesmen. While two lengths of three-eighths inch pipe can be twisted by strong hands, the twisters will do a better job. At Ascension Church, a do-it-yourselfer made a pair from hardwood. Although they did not have the strength of the ready-made metal ones (and would probably not last through another framework), they did the job.

Wooden Twisters:
FIGURE 8

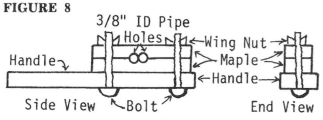

Figure 8 on this page is a diagram of these twisters. The handle measures 1" x ¾" x 20" and should be of strong wood. The two pieces of wood through which holes are bored to receive the three-eighths inch ID copper pipe must be the hardest wood available—at least as hard as maple. Each piece measures 3½" x 3/4" x 3/4" after planing smooth. The two pieces must fit perfectly where they butt.

Clamp the three pieces firmly together and drill (tight fit) for the wing nut bolts. Run the bolts through the handle and bottom piece of wood. Tighten the bolt with a nut sunk into the top of the bottom piece of maple. Add the top piece of maple, a washer, and wing nut. Tighten both bolts firmly. Drill the holes for a very tight fit of the three-eighths inch pipe. The edges of the holes should butt.

Jigs: FIGURE 9   **FIGURE 9**

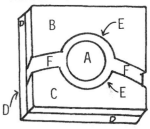

Wooden jigs simplify the shaping of the pipe to the pattern. Make them of three-fourths inch plywood. Circle A has the exact inside diameter of the season symbol circle. Two pieces, B and C, are nailed to a third piece, D. The E arcs are the outside line of the season symbol circles. The vine, twisted from two pieces of three-eighths inch copper pipe, lies inside the F paths. The actual working pattern determines the dimensions of these pieces. Note that circle A is not nailed to board D.

Make another jig, G, the size of an inside circle of a Trinity cycle cross, or 4½ inches in diameter, of three-fourths inch plywood.

DRAWING THE ACTUAL SIZE WORKING PATTERN

While the following instructions (unless otherwise noted) are specifically for laying out the pattern for the original framework, the procedure is the same for all other rigid frames. Adapt these directions to the scale drawing of the particular type framework that is wanted. Since these instructions are for full-size Chrismons, every measurement must be divided by two if the pattern is for half-size designs.

The full-size pattern requires an area about ten feet high by six feet wide. The bad sides of two four by eight foot pieces of plywood which are laid side by side with a two foot square piece at the center top make an excellent area on which to work. (Later, the plywood can be used for work on which only one side must be good.) If the area is smeared with green paint, it will be easier to judge the appearance of the work as it progresses.

Enlarge the diagrams which are described on page 12 under "Patterns" to make the actual size pattern. Because the diagrams are so small, they show only one line for the tubing. The pattern must show both sides of the pipe. Thus, for the Son circle, draw two circles—one for the inside edge of the frame and the other, three-eighths inch larger, for the outside.

Before any part of the pattern is drawn, practice, with the person who is to make the framework, bending the sizes of the copper tubing that will be used. Notice how much twist can be put into the pipe before it collapses; see how sharp a curve can be made before the tube flattens. The curls around the crosses at the ends of the vine are limited to what the pipe allows. A slight flattening of the pipe will not matter. But too much will seem unnatural and may even weaken the structure.

* * *

Start to sketch the pattern by drawing a vertical line down the center of the background. This line marks the center of the framework from the top Father circle, through the Pentecost circle, to below the cross crosslet. Draw a 4½ foot diameter circle, with its center on the center line and 2¾ feet above the bottom edge of the pattern area. The Life cycle is built on this circle. (For the Life cycle alone, point the top of the circle to make the teardrop shape.) Draw a 3½ foot diameter (three feet for the present frame) Trinity circle above the Life circle. These two circles, the Life and Trinity, must overlap at the Pentecost point; the length of the lap must be the exact inside diameter of a season circle, which is generally 8 1/8 inches.

This 8 1/8 inches is an exact measurement which must be coordinated between the Chrismon makers and the framework maker. It is the inside diameter of the decorative border into which each season symbol must fit. The framework must have exactly the same diameter as the circle around the season symbol so that the beadwork completely hides the tube. To insure a proper fit, the Chrismon makers must first make several beaded circles. (Very slight variations in bead size alter the completed circle's size. The worker cannot control this factor.) The framework maker must then make the diameter of his circles correspond to what has turned out in the construction of the Chrismons.

Draw in both sides of the Trinity circle (one-half inch for the original; three-eighths inch for the present). Draw the inside and outside lines for the season and Person circles. Note that, while the circles on the Life cycle are centered on the 4½ foot circle line, the Person circles are set two-thirds outside the Trinity cycle line (outside the line on the present framework). Draw in the circles (inside diameter, 4½ inches) which provide frames for the Cross Treflée and the Cross Flamant.

* * *

Now, study the pattern to see how the vine, which twists on itself, opens out to make the frames in which the Life cycle crosses hang. Since each cross has a different shape and hangs in a different relationship to the circle, this frame must be individually designed for each cross. Make paper cutouts to duplicate the finished crosses; then design the vine around them. The cutouts allow experimentation to find the best position for the crosses. Always place the cross to hang straight.

Begin the design of the vine around a cross. Draw the vine close enough to the cross to accent it. At the same time, curve and shape the vine so that it appears to grow naturally and to taper off, at the ends around the cross, into nothingness. This taper is achieved in the last few inches of the vine's construction by changing the three-eighths inch pipe to one-fourth inch pipe which is ended with a long diagonal cut. Practice bending of the tube demonstrates the capacity of the one-fourth inch pipe to bend more sharply than the three-eighths inch tubing.

Another factor governs the design of the vine around the crosses. When the Life cycle is made in sections, their tips are bolted together at the crosses. The cycle can be no stronger than the bolt that is run through the tip ends. If too large a hole is drilled, the tubing that remains will be too weak to maintain its shape; if the bolt is too small, it may break in use. (So that they will not be too noticeable, brass instead of silver colored bolts are used. Brass is not as sturdy as the silver metal.)

While a vine ended off like Detail B of Figure 10 below will look more graceful than Detail A, it will not have as much strength. Nothing is added to the sturdiness of the joint if one vine tip is like A and the other like B. The entire joint will be as weak as the B tip. The

FIGURE 10

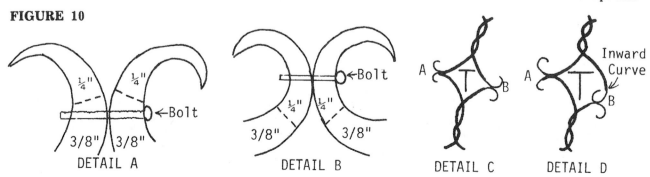

DETAIL A   DETAIL B   DETAIL C   DETAIL D

FRAMEWORK

B joint is strong enough to hold the circle even if it is used throughout. Ascension Church has used it, and it has held up over the years. But a sudden jolt in hanging or moving the framework may break it. If it is decided to use only the B joint, handle the framework with care.

Experience in making, handling, and hanging the framework leads to this suggestion: At each place where one section joins another, there are two bolting points. Make one an A type joint and the other, a B type, as shown on Detail C. Thus, there will be one strong joint at every cross around the circle.

Since three-eighths inch pipe will not curve as sharply as one-fourth inch pipe, try to use the A point at places where both tip ends curve outward. Detail D shows that the inward curve necessitates a sharper turn. Care in the design of the pattern makes it possible to have an A joint at every junction of the sections.

If the entire figure 8 is constructed in one unit, solder the joints together. In this case, joint B is sturdy enough to use throughout.

* * *

After the vine frames for the crosses are sketched, draw lines in which a double row of three-eighths inch pipe can lie for the twists which join the circles to the crosses. This six-eighths inch wide path for the twists should follow the 4½ foot circle line as closely as possible. Complete the vine by sketching grapes, leaves, and tendrils where they would naturally grow. Grapes HANG. Leaves may go up, down, or sideways. Tendrils go anywhere.

Sketch in the six and eight-point stars and censers to complete the actual working pattern.

CONSTRUCTION OF THE ORIGINAL RIGID FRAMEWORK

Construction of the framework on the actual size pattern makes it easy to shape the pattern pieces and to maintain the accuracy of the work as it progresses. The pattern is not only a guide but also a means of simplifying the job.

Each section of the Life cycle is constructed of fourteen pieces of copper pipe (preshaped or twisted) that are soldered together to fit the pattern. Figure 11 on this page shows these pieces and how they fit together. While Figure 11 is modeled after the Advent section, it is not a scale drawing. The two each A, C, and D pieces are three-eighths inch ID flexible or soft drawn pipe; pieces B, E, F, G, and H are one-fourth inch OD soft drawn pipe. The two A's are really one piece which is cut into two after the soldering has begun. Because the B's fit inside the A, C, and D pieces, only their corners show on the pattern. If a satisfactory bend can be made in the three-eighths inch pipe at M, construct the CAC and the DAD lengths in one piece. But if this is done, some interesting problems will develop in making the CD twist.

Measure, on the pattern, the length of C, the twist and part of the cross frame. Cut a piece of three-eighths inch tubing a couple of inches longer than the measurement. Measure and cut another piece of three-eighths inch pipe for D. Insert C and D in the twister. One twister is one-half inch from one end of the pieces; place the other twister so that the distance of the pipes between the twisters is equal to the length of the twist plus one-half inch. Practice enables one to judge the exact shrinkage in the twisting process and the number of turns that can be made before the tube flattens too much. Slight flattening will not matter. Lay the pipes, still in the twisters, directly over the pattern. Make any necessary curve in the twist. With the hands or with tools if desired, shape the individual curves that form the frame for the cross. Remove the pipes from the twisters. Place the tubing lengths over the pattern again to check the fit. Cut off the ends of the pipes to fit. (If the twisters are good enough, it may be possible to place one twister at the ends of the pipes. But it is generally better to cut the ends off to fit the pattern.)

Place C and D back in the twisters. At the center back of the twist, solder the C and D pieces together. This may not be what one would call a good soldered joint. But if enough flux is used in the turns of the twist, the joint will do the job required of it. (Throughout these directions, an experienced solderer may shudder at some of the methods. But we wanted a certain effect; these directions explain how we got it. They W O R K. Maybe you can figure out a better way. If it gives the desired effect and if it results in a durable framework, use it.)

Fit, twist, shape, and solder the opposite CD pipes.

* * *

From three-eighths inch tubing, shape a complete A circle around jig A, which is explained on Figure 9. Also see Figure 12 on

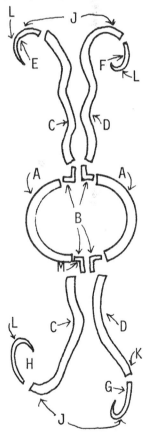

FIGURE 11

FRAMEWORK

FIGURE 12

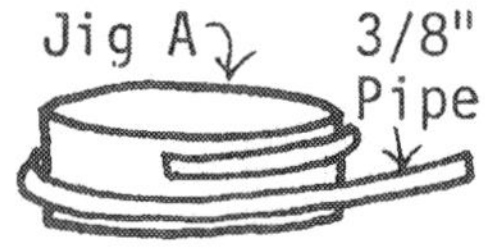

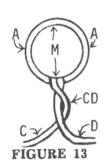

FIGURE 13

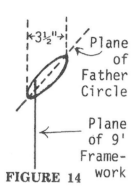

FIGURE 14

FIGURE 15

page 16. Cut a piece, generally five to six-eighths inch, out of the circle so that the CD twist will fit into the circle. See M on Figure 13 at the left.

Two B pieces, each of which is a four inch piece of one-fourth inch pipe bent at a right angle in the middle, join the circle to the twist. Cover a B piece liberally with flux; place one end of B in an open end of circle A; place the other end of B in C. Use another B to similarly join the other open end of A to D. Solder the two B pieces into the CD twist and the open A ends at the same time. Run some solder to join the B's at their angles. After soldering the joint at the lower M point shown on Figure 13, cut a space out of A to accept the CD section at the upper M point. Solder the upper CD twist into the circle.

Stop a moment to consider how the framework will look on the tree. See pages 11 and 21. Depending on the tree's height, the Advent circle will be about ten feet from the floor; the Father circle will be fifteen feet up; the Lenten circle will be about 6½ feet high. The entire nine foot framework will be at an angle slanted to face the ceiling. If the congregation is to see the symbols easily, especially the Person symbols, they must be tilted toward the floor of the nave. Fortunately, this is more simply done than explained. Do not tilt the 3½ and 4½ foot cycles—just the season and Person circles. Angle these circles independently of and contrary to the plane of the cycles. See Figure 14 at the above left. The degree of tilt depends on the height of the circle above the floor. While the Father circle should be tilted about three inches if it is fifteen feet above the floor, the Pentecost circle on the same framework would be tilted only one-and-one-half or two inches; the Lenten circle only about one-half inch if at all.

The framework maker must remember to put the proper tilt on each circle as he or she fits and constructs it. Angle the circles to the cycles either by the way the CD twist is soldered to A or by bending the twists or by shaping the circle after it is joined to the vine. Or use a combination of these adjustments. After tilting the circle, check the whole CD-CD assembly by the pattern.

The one-fourth inch pipe end sections—E, F, G, and H—consist of what appears in the pattern plus about two inches which is slipped into the end of the C or D pipe and soldered in place. The end of the one-fourth inch pipe is cut off diagonally to make a tapered end. If no leaf or bunch of grapes is on the tip (G), solder is melted into the end to close the hole. Later, the end is filed off smooth to finish the peak.

To attach grapes or a leaf at the end (E, F, and H), leave the diagonal hole at the end open. After the framework is on the tree, insert the wire stem of the grapes or the leaf into the diagonal hole on the end; continue the stem through a hole drilled in the side wall of the one-fourth inch tubing (L on Figure 15 on this page). Pull the leaf or grape bunch tight against the diagonal hole. Curl the leftover stem wire that emerges from hole L to form a tendril. The curl holds the leaf or grapes in place. (To form a tendril, wrap the wire evenly and closely around a half inch dowel. About three inches from the end of the stem, slip the dowel out and continue to wrap the wire around a pencil point to end off the curl.)

When a leaf is attached to the vine at a place other than the end, drill completely through both walls of the tubing. After the stem is run through the tube, arrange the leaf on one side of the vine and curl the excess stem wire to make a tendril on the other. Again the curl holds the leaf in place. (K on Figure 11.)

Cut, shape, and fit E, F, G, and H; finish the ends and/or drill holes according to the attachments to be made on them. Then, cover the end of E liberally with flux; slip it into the end of C to fit the pattern; solder it in place. Build up solder around the outside of the joint so that it can be filed off to appear naturally tapered. Solder and file F, G, and H. Drill through D at K for holes for a leaf stem.

The Advent section is complete! Advent will join Christmas at the lower J points on Figure 11. Notice that one J is on three-eighths inch pipe and the other on one-fourth inch pipe. Make the other season sections in the same way as the Advent section. Finally, make the two vine sections that come out from each side of the Pentecost circle.

File and polish all the soldered joints smooth. Check all the sections against the pattern. Each must touch the next to it at the J points. Be sure that each cross has enough space in its vine frame. Check the tilt of the season circles. Make any necessary adjustments.

Drill the bolt holes through points J. Use two sizes of bolts and holes—one for the one-fourth inch pipes and a larger one for the three-eighths inch pipes. Bolt the sections together to recheck them against the pattern.

FRAMEWORK

To finish the framework in one piece, cut the bolts off short. Run solder around the bolted joints to strengthen them except at St. Andrew's and Constantine's Crosses. Join these places after the Trinity cycle is added.

Place the finished crosses, with their hanging wires attached, in position. On the back of the cross frame, screw short (three-eighths to one-half inch) metal screws in the best position to provide places at which the crosses can hang after the framework is on the tree. Do not screw through the vine—just enough into it to hold the screw firmly.

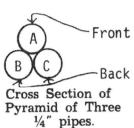

Cross Section of Pyramid of Three ¼" pipes.

FIGURE 16

Begin construction of the original Trinity circle by shaping three-eighths inch pipe around jig A. (See "Jigs" on page 13.) Cut off the pipe to make an exact circle. Cover the cut and inner edges of the circle with flux. Put a one inch piece of one-fourth inch flux covered pipe and a few pieces of solder inside the end of the circle. Close the circle and clamp it with the cut down so that gravity keeps the one-fourth inch pipe and solder at the cut. Solder the circle closed. Cut and solder the other Person and the Pentecost circles in the same manner. Shape the cross circles on jig G; solder them closed.

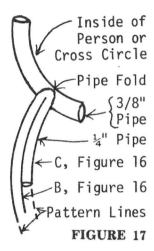

FIGURE 17

FIGURE 18

The 3½ foot Trinity circle line is constructed of sections of a pyramid of three one-fourth inch pipes. See Figure 16 at the top left. Each section runs from the inside edge of one circle to the inside edge of the next circle in the cycle. These arcs run between 1) and the Cross Flamant and the Son, 2) the Son and the Father, 3) the Father and the Spirit, and 4) the Spirit and the Cross Treflee. Construction of two more arcs, each of which connects to the Pentecost circle, varies slightly.

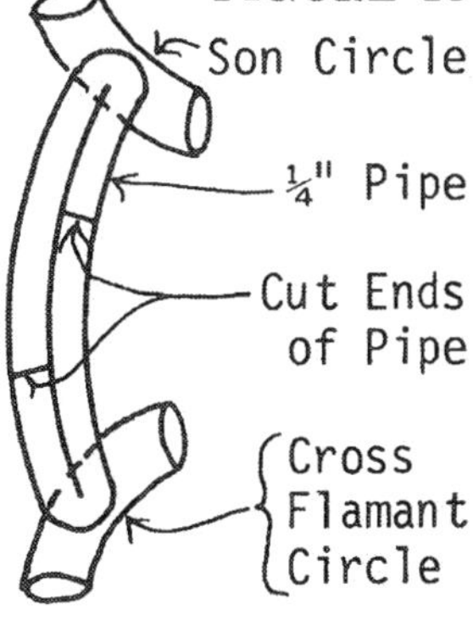

Cut a length of one-fourth inch pipe about equal to the length of the section that is to be built.

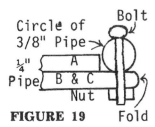

FIGURE 19

Fold the pipe about one-third the distance from one end so that the two ends run in the same direction. Hammer the fold so that it is level with the unfolded pipe diameter. Place the fold at the inside edge of the circle pattern at one end of the arc; shape the two free ends of the pipe to follow the pattern. See Figure 17 at the left. Fit, fold, and shape another length of one-fourth inch tubing to fit from the inside edge of the circle at the other end of the arc to the free ends of the first one-fourth inch pipe. The cut ends of the tubing must NOT lie opposite each other. See Figure 18 at the left.

Shape and cut another piece of one-fourth inch pipe, A on Figure 16, to fit in the groove between B and C. A butts the outside edges of the circles which the pyramid, of which A is a part, connects. See A on Figure 19 at the left.

With nuts and bolts, fasten the pyramid, of which A is a part, together. Bolt B to C, C to A, and A to B. Space the bolts along the length of the arc. Position them so that the nut is least noticeable from the floor when the framework is on the tree. Further, arrange the bolts so that one connects the B and C tubes at the point directly behind the bowl of the chalice and another behind the middle of the shell. The heads of these two bolts (each of which should be at least 1¾ inches long) should be on the inside of the Trinity cycle with the nut end running outside the circle and at right angles to it. These will be the attachment points for the stars. Cut off the ends of all the other bolts even with the nuts. These other bolts will also serve as attachment points for the pearls and censers when the framework is on the tree.

Bolt the cross and Person circles to the arcs. In the bolting, tilt the circle to its proper angle to the plane of the whole Trinity cycle. See Figure 14 on page 16 and Figure 19 on this page.

Since even the smallest bolt that can be used weakens the arc, run enough solder around the nuts and bolts to regain the predrilled strength of the tubing. (Because it stands up from its supports, the Trinity cycle must have more strength than the Life cycle.)

The sections of the Trinity cycle between the crosses and the Pentecost circle are made like the other arcs except that, at the Pentecost circle end, A, B, and C end in open tubing. Thus, all of B and C are made from one piece of one-fourth inch pipe which is folded where it joins the cross circle. Make the ends of A, B, and C about an inch longer than needed where they run into Pentecost. Do not put any solder or bolts in the last inch of the arc where it joins the Pentecost circle. DO NOT attach the arcs to the Pentecost circle at this time.

The Trinity and Life cycles are now complete. It remains to attach both to the Pentecost circle. At the same time that this is done, the supports by which the whole Series hangs are made. To understand the strength necessary in this construction, stop to read the directions for hanging a rigid framework on page 21.

The whole Christian Year Series on the rigid framework hangs from two projections. Each of these supports is made of two pieces of one-fourth inch pipe (from B and C of the Trinity cycle), one piece of three-eighths inch tube (from the upper piece of the vine twist), and wires and solder to hold them together. This complex of pipes, wire, and solder must fit into a one inch ID pipe. On each side of the Pentecost circle, an A of the Trinity cycle and a lower piece of the vine twist continue under the Pentecost circle to its inside diameter where they are cut off. Thus, these pieces help to support the Pentecost circle and may even be slightly bent to fit the tilt of the circle. But these pieces do not go into the projections.

The projections, by which the whole Series hangs, extend directly behind the Pentecost circle where the vine and Trinity cycles meet. Their position is such that the beaded circle around the seven-tongued flame almost hides them from view. The projections are perpendicular to the plane of the whole double loop—NOT perpendicular to the Pentecost circle, which must be tilted as explained on Figure 14 on page 16. So that the angle of this turn has as much strength as possible, use 90° copper elbow fittings on each pipe that goes into the projection.

The actual construction of the right angle turn from the Trinity cycle and the vine into the projection is a matter of careful fitting. Lay the Trinity cycle and upper pieces of the vine over the pattern; position the Pentecost circle; then note where the Trinity cycle and vine ends must be cut to allow the projections to extend directly behind the Pentecost circle.

It generally works out that the A's of the Trinity cycle and the lower twists of the vine are cut at the Pentecost circle's inside diameter line. Although these pieces do not make the turn into the projection, they are behind the circle to be soldered to it. Thus, they add to the strength of the junction of the two cycles to the circle. Bend these ends slightly to provide the foundation for the proper tilt of the Pentecost circle which was described on Figure 14 on page 16.

B and C of the Trinity cycle and the upper twist of the vine go into the ninety degree elbows which make the turn into the projections. Generally, these pipes should be cut at the outside diameter line of the Pentecost circle or about one-fourth inch closer to the center of the circle. Insert straight five to six inch lengths of the proper size pipe in the open ends of the elbows. The cuts in the vine and the B and C ends will probably be at different points to allow the elbows to make the turns so that the straight pieces that form the projections lie close together.

If the turn is fitted so that one or more of the elbows touch the Pentecost circle, the joint will be stronger.

After the joint is cut and fitted satisfactorily, assemble it for soldering. Use flux liberally in the assembly. To strengthen the joint and to help hold it during the soldering process, run a bolt (from front to back) through the Pentecost circle into and through one of the vine twists. Screw a nut on the back of the bolt tightly. Twist a wire tightly around the Pentecost circle and B and C to hold them in place. Twist and spiral a wire around the three pipes of each projection to hold the pipes closely together. Check to be sure that the projections will fit inside two parallel one inch ID pipes. Solder liberally at all points of contact to make a strong series of joints. After the soldering is complete, check to see that each projection will still slide into its parallel pipe. If too much solder has built up on either projection, file it off.

Because it is easier to build the projections without handling the whole Life cycle, joining the cycle at the frames of St. Andrew's and Constantine's Crosses was delayed. Make those connections now by bolting and/or soldering them.

Finally, spray the whole framework gold with the best quality gold spray paint that can be found. Paint the two projections the same green that is used on the pipes and blocks of wood which are used to mount the framework on the tree. See page 22.

The original framework is finished! If it is properly constructed, the framework can be supported at the projections or at any place on the Trinity cycle including the circles of that cycle. While the Life cycle is not as strong, it is sturdy enough to do the work required of it.

* * *

This construction is not an easy job. The work is exacting and tedious. But it is within the ability of even a first-time solderer. Many people have done it without any professional help. The detail in the directions should not deter anyone from attempting the rigid framework. The detail is there for the same reason that it is in other Chrismon directions—to insure that those who begin the job will have the know-how to see it through.

Once the framework is made, it can be used year after year. The time that it saves every Christmas when the tree is decorated (and during this season, time is a valuable commodity) will make up for the hours spent in construction. Most important of all, the effect of the Series on the rigid framework on the tree is so superior to hanging the Series directly on the branches that, at least for Ascension Church, this factor alone makes the construction of the rigid framework worth-while.

FRAMEWORK

FIGURE 20
Not to Scale

SIMPLIFIED RIGID FRAMEWORK

FIGURE 21
(Scale Drawing)
(1" to 1')

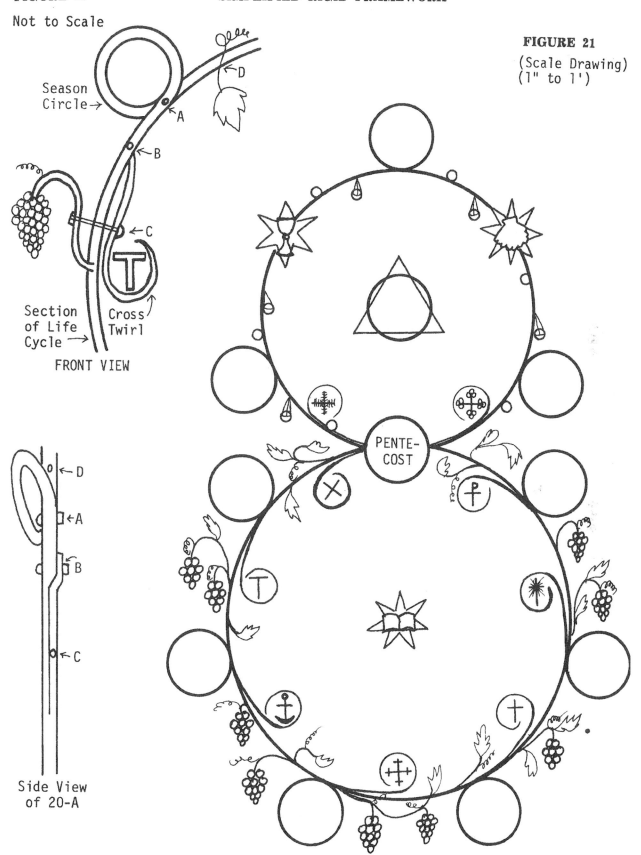

CONSTRUCTION OF SIMPLIFIED FRAMEWORKS

Directions for the original framework cover all facets of rigid framework building. The following instructions explain only how to simplify some original procedures. Consequently, one must study the original framework directions before these adaptations can be used.

The pictures and diagrams show several ways to simplify the framework. But one need not follow any method in its entirety. Read all the directions to note the various possibilities. Then, combine them in any desired manner.

SIMPLIFICATION by Figure 21 on Page 19:

Begin at the left side of the Pentecost circle. Shape three-eighths inch pipe to the cycle from Pentecost to St. Andrew's Cross. (Use one-fourth inch pipe for the half-size.) Shape the pipe around jig G ("Jigs" on page 13) to make the circle for St. Andrew's Cross. (Figures 20 A and B on page 19 show this loop.) Continue the pipe to the Advent circle; form that circle around jig A. Continue to shape the pipe around the Life cycle to the right side of Pentecost. Bend the pipe as each circle is lapped to give that circle its proper "tilt."

Make the Trinity cycle in like manner. Begin at the left of the Pentecost circle; shape the cycle with its circles around to the right of Pentecost. This is the present Trinity cycle.

Or to give a vine-like appearance to the Life cycle, make it of two three-eighths inch pipes. Twist them on themselves from Pentecost to St. Andrew's Cross. Then, shape the frame for the cross on only one pipe. Continue the twist of both pipes to the Advent circle, which is also shaped on only one tube. Continue twisting and shaping the pipe to the Pentecost circle. To strengthen the cycle, run solder between the pipes and behind each twisted section.

After the cycle is made by either above procedure, run a bolt through both pipes where the circle pipe crosses over itself. See points A on Figures 20. Tighten the nut; cut off any excess bolt length. Run solder around the joint to strengthen it and file it smooth.

B and C on Figures 20 A and B show how grape and leaf attachments, of one-fourth inch pipe, are bolted to the Life cycle. Taper the ends of added pipes by diagonal cutting, hammering, solder filling, and/or filing. Whenever a bolt is used, run it so that it is least noticeable from the floor when the framework is on the tree. Leaves and grapes may also be attached by drilling small holes through the three-eighths inch pipe as shown at the D's on Figures 20 A and B.

Follow the original directions for making the projections, each of which is composed of two three-eighths inch pipes. Attach the Pentecost circle by running a bolt through each side of the circle, from the inside out, and into the front of each projection.

SIMPLIFICATION by Front Cover Picture:

Use two pieces of three-eighths inch pipe, one thirty feet long, the other forty-two feet in length. (Half-size: Use one-fourth inch pipe, one piece sixteen feet long, the other twenty-two feet.) Eight inches from the end of both pipes, begin to twist the pieces together while shaping them to the five foot diameter Life cycle. When the twisted Life cycle is complete, continue the tubes (side by side, not twisted) around the 3½ foot diameter Trinity cycle. When the figure 8 is complete, continue the longer tube around the Trinity cycle again so that the longer tube forms a pyramid with the first two tubes. Cut off the pipes so that the leftover ends are eight inches long.

The upper loop of the figure 8 is now a pyramid of three pipes like Figure 16 on page 17; the lower loop is two pieces of pipe twisted on each other. Each of the four pipe ends at the crossover is eight inches long. Figure 22 on this page pictures the front of the crossover point; Figure 23 shows how the tubing is bent at the back to go into two hanging projections of two three-eighths inch pipes each.

FIGURE 22   **FIGURE 23**

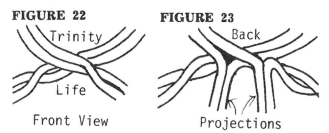

Front View   Projections

At the point where a season or Person circle touches the cycle, drill two holes, about one-half inch apart, in the pipes of the cycle. Make the hole big enough to accept a 10 or 12 gauge copper wire. Solder an end of a length of the wire in one hole. Shape the wire from the hole twice around jig A. Remove the jig. Continue the wire around the circle of two wires; but this time, wrap the wire around the previously made circles to hold them firmly together. Cut off the excess wire; solder the remaining end in the other hole in the pipe to hold the attached circle in place.

Make the cross twirls and leaf and grape stems by soldering ends of 10 or 12 gauge copper wires in holes drilled in the cycle tubing. Two wires may be set in the same hole. Curve the wire to the desired shape; cut it off to fit the pattern. Cover the wire with a length of plastic clothesline from which the core is removed. Cut off the ends of the clothesline diagonally. See page 23 for a description of the clothesline and directions on how to mount the accessories on and into the clothesline.

This is, by far, the easiest method of rigid framework construction.

FRAMEWORK

HANGING THE RIGID FRAMEWORK ON THE TREE

When one uses the rigid framework, the entire Christian Year Series hangs on two projections, each of which is about seven-eighths of an inch in diameter and six inches long. These supports emerge from the framework where the Life vine and the Trinity pyramid join the Pentecost circle. See Figure 24 on this page. (When the Series is divided to hang on two trees, the projections extend behind the Pentecost circle at its junction with the Life cycle and behind the Father circle at its junction with the Trinity cycle.)

The framework is actually hung on the tree by pushing the two projections into the open ends of two pipes. These two pipes are attached, at their opposite ends, to the trunk of the tree. This is done in such a way that the double loop seems to rest on the branches just as ordinary ornaments would appear if they were hung directly on the tree. See Figure 25 on page 21. The entire job is simply accomplished with two pipes, two blocks of wood, two guy wires, and a few nails and bolts.

The two pipes can be either ordinary one inch cast iron or thin wall conduit or telescoping poles. The pipes should be about three feet longer than the widest possible distance between the trunk of the tree and the outer edge of the tree's branches at the height of the Pentecost circle.

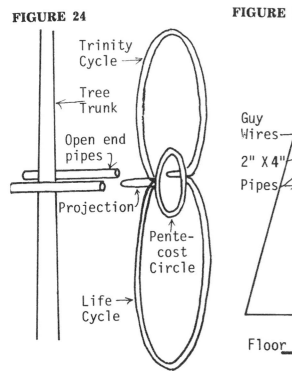

FIGURE 24

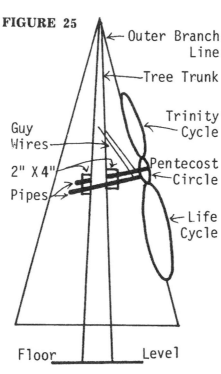

FIGURE 25

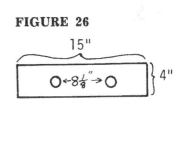

FIGURE 26

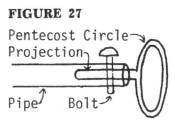

FIGURE 27

You must estimate this measurement for your tree. Drill holes to accept the guy wires through the front ends of the pipes.

Each of the two like blocks of wood is two by four by about fifteen inches. See Figure 26 on page 21. In each block of wood, drill two holes to tightly accept the one inch pipe. Since the distance between the holes must be the exact distance between the projections on which the double loop is hung, the holes cannot be drilled until the framework is made. Paint the blocks of wood and the pipes a dark green so that they will be unobtrusive when the tree is decorated.

Attach the pipes to the tree before hanging any decorations. The pounding necessary to hang the pipes would knock off or disarrange any ornaments or lights on the tree. First, decide on the placement of the Pentecost circle. It must be at the place on the circumference of the tree where it can be seen from the most seats in the room. Figures 4, 5, 6, and 7 on pages 11 and 12 will help to decide on the height.

Run the pipes through the holes in one of the blocks of wood. Insert the pipes through the branches of the tree so that the poles are on opposite sides of the trunk, the block of wood next to the trunk and in front of it, and the ends of the pipe through which the guy wire holes were drilled at the front edge of the branches at the exact point where the Pentecost circle will be. The pipes are NOT perpendicular to the trunk of the tree; they are perpendicular to the outer branch line of the tree where the Pentecost circle will hang. Notice the angles shown on Figure 25. When the pipes are pushed through the branches from the Pentecost point to the trunk of the tree, they are slanted downward. Thereafter, someone must hold the two pipes in place at the Pentecost point throughout the process of attaching them to the tree.

When the position of the pipes is satisfactory, nail the block of wood to the front of the tree. Slip the other drilled wood over the pipes from the back to the tree trunk. Nail the second block in place to the back of the trunk. These two pieces of wood should hold the pipes in place. But to add an extra margin of safety, run guy wires from the holes bored for them in the pipes up to the trunk of the tree as shown on Figure 25.

Adjustable, telescoping poles are easier to use than the pipes. (Sears' catalogue lists tent canopy poles which are the right diameter. If they are too long, cut off their ends.) If the pipes have a knob on the ends, counter sink the holes on one block of wood to accept the knobs. Slip the wood over the poles to the ends. Then nail a thin piece of wood over the ends of the poles to hold them in place.

When these poles are put into the tree to straddle the trunk, they must be pushed up from the back toward the Pentecost position. Slip the front block over the poles; nail the blocks to the trunk. Adjusting the ends of the poles to the surface of the tree is a simple matter of pulling a pole out or pushing it in and turning it to lock it into position.

To hang the double loop, merely push the projections into the open pipe ends. Because of the tilt on the pipes, gravity holds the framework in place. Check to see that the double loop follows the surface of the branches of the tree. If it is too far out or in, remove the framework and drive the pipes further into or out of the middle of the tree. Hammer blows squarely on the pipe ends will do the job.

Also check to see that the whole double loop follows the surface on the tree. Sometimes, branches jut out at one or two places. If this is the case, prune them to make an even background for the framework. If there are deep holes in the tree or if the tree is slim and the framework wide, parts of either cycle may stand too far out in the air. Practically any part of the cycles may be bent to follow the shape of the tree even though the framework is completely built. But the only person who should do this bending is the one who built it. He or she knows where to adjust the shape without weakening the structure. Everyone must accept the builder's judgment as to when the framework is best fitted to the tree. In any event, it is better to make adjustments by pruning the tree rather than bending the framework.

After the fitting of the framework to the tree is completed, remove the framework and set it aside. Decorate the tree above the framework position; place the lights (if they are used) over the area where the framework will fit. Then, replace the framework and decorate it with its symbols, crosses, and accessories.

While gravity will hold the framework in place, it may be better to make an extra attachment. Either tightly twist a heavy wire in a figure 8 around and between the guy wires and the Pentecost circle at the projections; or before the pipes and double loop are placed on the tree, drill for a one-eighth inch bolt through the pipe and projections. After the framework has been hung, drop the bolt in place as shown on Figure 27 on page 21.

FRAMEWORK

FLEXIBLE CONNECTIONS: Construction & Hanging

When the Christian Year Series hangs directly on the branches of a tree, flexible pieces which hang from the symbols themselves show the relationship of each Chrismon to the next in the cycle. On the Life cycle, these connections look like a vine. Since there are seven season symbols, seven sections of vine connect them. On the Trinity cycle, three connections join the Person circles to one another.

Hanging the symbols on the tree so that they give the effect of the two cycles in the sketch will not be easy. But with care, the proper relationship between the parts of the Series can be shown. Because one cannot be certain of the distance between the Chrismons before they are on the tree, it is best to make the connections longer than may be needed. The excess length can be folded behind a Chrismon or draped gracefully. But if a section is too short, it cannot be stretched. Make each vine section about one yard long and each Trinity braid about one and one-fourth yards in length.

* * *

Page 21 shows the Life twists with some season symbols; a closer view of a Life twist and a Trinity braid is on page 22. These particular connections were made of plastic clothesline, an inexpensive material. But it may not be suitable for the full-size Series because it is not generally available in a large enough diameter, which should be almost one-half inch. If it is used, try to get the kind with fiber AND wire filler. Hobby shops which sell materials for model airplanes have a transparent plastic tubing in sizes from one-fourth to one-half inch. While this tubing gives the desired size, finish, and flexibility, it is comparatively expensive. Heavy cord or light rope meets some of the requirements for the vine material. But its appearance will be dull even after it is sprayed several times with a metallic gold paint. Wire is too stiff to hang gracefully. However, careful placement on the tree may make it acceptable in spite of its weight. Although it is expensive, heavy metallic gold braid may also be used. Personal experimentation is the only way to decide which material is preferred.

To make each braid, start with three lengths of clothesline a little longer than the desired finished braid. Sew them together at one end; braid them (most people learned to braid when they were children); then sew the ends together so that the braid does not unravel.

To make the vine sections, use another grammar school trick. Let a person at one end twist a seven foot length of clothesline in one direction while another, at the other end, turns the line in the opposite direction. When the line is tightly twisted, a third person takes it in the middle to start it to twist automatically on itself. The whole length will curl around itself to give the effect of a twisting vine. Pin the ends to hold them in place until they can be sewn together.

Points of attachment to the vine for the leaves and grapes are pieces, about 2½ inches long, of the clothesline with the ends cut off diagonally. Remove the core from the plastic line with tweezers. (Wire and fiber core is recommended because it is easier to pull out than the solid fiber core.) Attach about three of the tubing pieces to each vine section by placing the diagonal cut against a twist of the vine and sewing it in place so that it appears to be a growing stem.

Clothesline, with the core removed, also serves as the circular cross frames. Twist one end of a 16½ inch length of about fourteen gauge wire around the hole in the end of a small, gold safety pin. Shape the wire to a 4½ inch diameter circle. Run a 14½ inch length of decored clothesline over the wire circle. Run the end of the wire through the safety pin hole; twist the wire to hold the circle closed. Cut off the excess wire.

* * *

Spray the braids, vine sections, and cross frames with thin coats of a good quality metallic gold paint. Allow plenty of drying time between the coats of paint.

* * *

Attach the grapes by inserting the wire stem of a bunch through the open end of an attachment piece of tubing. Run the wire through the stem length to the vine twist. Push the grape stem wire through one of the vine twists, wrap it around the twist to hold it in place, and curl the excess wire to form a tendril.

Fasten the leaves to the stem attachments by folding a leaf stem end to fit inside the open tubing end. Cover the folded stem with glue and push it into the open end of the stem attachment.

Center the crosses in the circle frames with the top of the cross directly below the safety pin hanger. Thread the hanging wires through needles and sew the wires through the clothesline so that the cross is held in its proper position. Twist the hanger wires around themselves to anchor them. Cut off the excess wire.

* * *

To decorate the tree, hang the season and Person symbols to duplicate, as nearly as possible, the diagram of the Christian Year Series on page 1. Next, attach the connections from one symbol to the next with little gold safety pins; pin the connections to the borders of the symbols. The braid which joins the Son to the Spirit dips behind the top of the Pentecost circle to join the two cycles. Hang the shell over the braid between the Father and the Spirit, the chalice over the Father to Son braid. Next, pin the cross circles to their proper connections so that the crosses hang straight. Finally, space the censers and pearls on the Trinity braids.

SEASON & PERSON BORDERS

To show that each symbol is part of the same story, the gold glass bead circles around the original season and Person symbols are all alike. Beads are woven to give the appearance of a circle of light. Their design suggests the aureole and glory frequently seen around depictions of any person of the Triune in art. However, such usage is not customary on pictures of our Lord in His State of Humiliation. While this was known when the original Series was made, it was felt that all the circles should be alike.

Since these borders are not difficult to construct, the original ones are generally used for the simplified Series. Still, a less expensive and easier circle is also suggested.

Over the years, some Chrismon makers wanted more durable borders than glass beads made possible. But the holes in metal beads were too small for the heavy wire needed to support the circle. A few workers drilled each bead to enlarge the hole to make the metal beads usable.

More recently, it was decided to design borders specifically for metal beads. At the same time, the square was substituted for the "glory peaks" on the borders of the season symbols. The square, a symbol for the earth, was woven into and around the circle, an echo of the Son's divinity, to depict His dual nature. Thus, this present design uses a circle-square combination to show God's action in the world through His Son (in the Life cycle) and through the Spirit on Pentecost. The circles for both the Person and season symbols are alike. But while the square is combined with the circle on the season symbols, peaks to suggest the "glory" are woven out from the Person and Trinity circles.

NOTE: Slight variations in bead size alter circle sizes. Several borders MUST be woven before any symbols are made to fit them. Adjustment in the symbol patterns or the design of the circle may be necessary.

ORIGINAL GLASS BEAD CIRCLES

These directions are only for thin glass beads or metal beads with enlarged holes. See the photograph of the phoenix on page 38 for a close-up view of this border.

Materials: Light coat hangers; #30 gold hair wire; gold glass beads. (Different patterns which employ various size beads may be used.)

Directions:

Construction of the original circles for the Christian Year Series is similar to making the circle for the "Fish in a Circle" in the Basic Series. For the Fish, an extra row of beads is woven on #30 wire inside the heavy, beaded frame wire. For the Christian Year circles, two extra rows are woven on two extra #30 wires—one for a row of beads inside the beads on the heavy circle wire and the other for beaded peaks outside the main circle.

Use gold or light-colored wire about the weight of light wire coat hangers for the circle frame. (Bronze-colored hangers went into the original Chrismons.) Bend one end of a 30 inch length of wire to the triangular shape shown at A on Detail 1, Figure 28 on page 25. Then curve the wire to an 8½ inch diameter circle. The circle end will lap over itself a few inches. Shape the circle carefully before any beads are strung. Correcting irregularities in the wire after beads are on it will cause the heavy wire to crush the comparatively delicate glass beads.

* * *

Loop, twist, and anchor the middle of a 36 inch length of #30 wire around the frame wire at point B on Detail 2 of Figure 28. Run a 10 mm bead over the frame wire and both #30 wire ends. Bend one #30 wire end to the inside of the circle; run a 6 or 8 mm bead on it; push the 8 mm (hereafter called the 8 mm even though it can be either 6 or 8 mm) bead close to the 10 mm bead. Hold the free end of the #30 wire at the frame; twist the 8 mm bead on the wire so that it holds close to the 10 mm bead on the circle. Run another 10 mm bead over all three wires; push it against the previous 10 mm bead.

Bend one #30 wire to the outside of the circle, the other to the inside. Place and twist an 8 mm bead on the inside wire. String a 10 mm bead over the inside wire and the circle wire. Add another 8 mm bead on the inside #30 wire and twist it in place. Run three 6 mm beads on the outside #30 wire; add a gold seed bead. Twist the seed bead on the #30 wire to hold it close to the other beads on the wire. Add three more 6 mm beads on the outside wire. Run a 10 mm bead over all three wires; pull all the wires tight. Twist an 8 mm bead on the inside of the circle, string another 10 mm bead over all three wires; twist an 8 mm bead inside the circle. On the outer wire, string a 10, 8, and 6 mm bead in that order. Place a seed bead on the wire; run the #30 wire back through the 6, 8, and 10 mm beads. Hold the #30 wire firmly; twist the seed bead at the end to anchor it close to the others on the projection. One unit of the circle is now woven. The complete circle consists of 12 units just like this.

Note: When a projection of several beads is made, anchor only the last bead or those marked C on the pattern. The drawing shows beads loosely placed so that the wires can be seen; when weaving beads, keep the wires tight—especially when twisting a bead to anchor it in place. When the #30 wire is used up, attach another piece at any single-line projection. Hook

BORDERS

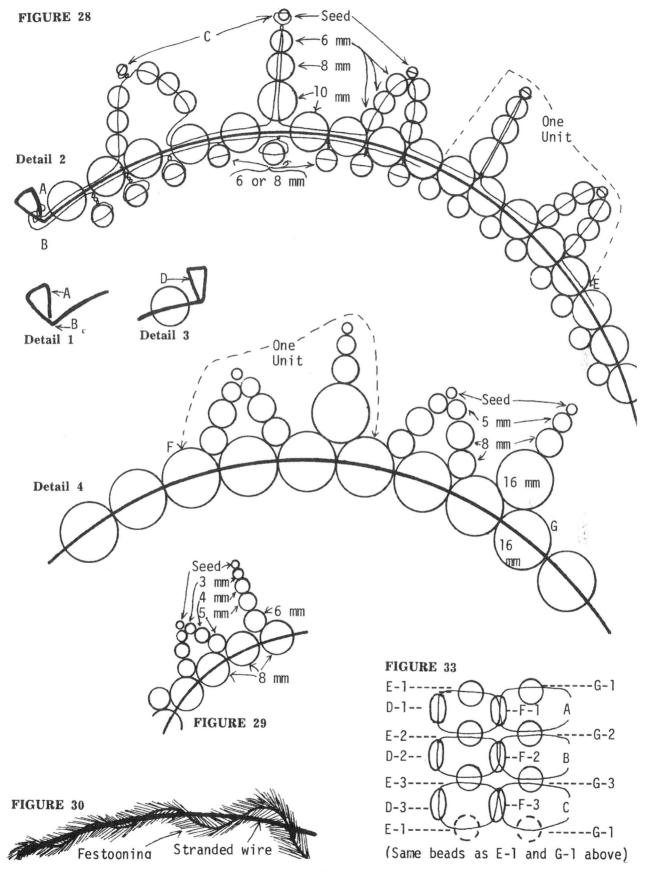

FIGURE 28

FIGURE 29

FIGURE 30

FIGURE 33

and twist the new wire around the last projection. Then use the new wire along with the last of the old wire to bead the circle until both wires twist on the next projection. Cut off the remnant of the old wire.

When the circle is complete (except for the last projections), bend the frame wire to make triangle D on Detail 3 which is like triangle A. Use strong pliers to keep the pressure off the beads. Cut off the excess frame wire. Twist the #30 wire around the triangles to hold them together. Then weave the last inner and outer projections in front of the triangles. The excess #30 wire becomes the hanger.

* * *

Detail 4 of Figure 28 shows, between F and G, a simplified pattern for a gold bead circle. This method uses one #30 wire to weave projections on the outside of the circle only. (The 5 mm beads are metal instead of glass.)

Either design AE or FG may be used for the original circles. Or create your own design to fit the bead sizes that you have. Just be sure to have enough projections from the circle to make it look like a sun rather than a star.

* * *

For rigid frameworks, attach the ends of three pieces of #30 wire to the circle frame at three points on the circle. Attach the symbol to the framework with these three wires.

ORIGINAL HALF or HOME-SIZE CIRCLES

Shape a 4 1/8 inch circle of 20 gauge copper wire. Bead the circle in a pattern like or similar to the one shown on Figure 29 on page 25. Extra beads are woven only on one wire outside the base circle. The 8 and 6 mm beads may be metal or glass; the 3, 4, and 5 mm beads must be metal. This border is pictured on page 21.

SIMPLIFIED CIRCLE BORDER

If a less expensive border is wanted, make it of stranded wire wrapped with 1½ inch gold vinyl festooning. To allow enough clearance inside the fringed circle for the symbols, shape the wire to a 8 7/8 inch diameter circle. (The fringe extends farther into the circle than the woven beads.) Spiral festooning around the wire as shown on Figure 30 on page 25. Fasten the ends of the festooning to the wire with transparent sticky tape. More complete directions for this circle are in the Basic book under the "Iota Chi woven through two Circles."

WOVEN METAL BEAD BORDERS

Use metal beads only. Pictures of the full-size season border with the Flames and the full-size Dove in a Person circle are on this page.

Materials: #14 stiff, green florist wire; #30 gold hair wire; 3, 4, 5, 6, and 3 x 6 mm gold metal beads.

Directions:

Circles for the Person and season symbols are alike. These woven triangular tubes are 6 mm gold metal beads on the lengthwise wires and 3 x 6 ovals on the crossover wires. After the weave on #30 wire is completed, a #14 green florist wire is pushed through the length of the weave; then the wire and weave are bent to a circle. Finally the weave is closed by running the #30 wire ends through the start of the tube weave.

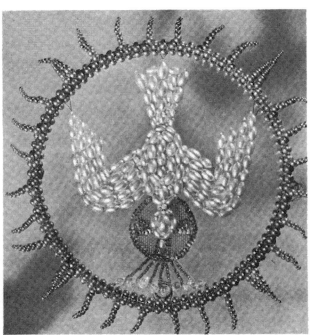

BORDERS

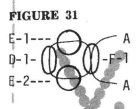

FIGURE 31

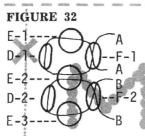

FIGURE 32

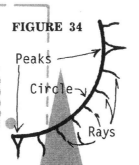

FIGURE 34

Peaks
Circle
Rays

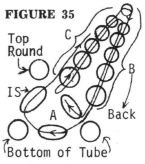

FIGURE 35

Top Round
IS
Back
Bottom of Tube

To weave the whole circle on one set of wires, begin with three 9 foot lengths of #30 wire. If such lengths are too unwieldy, begin with three 5 foot wires. (Put in new 5 foot wires after EXACTLY half the circle is woven; cut out the leftover first wires after no more than two loops of double wires. Mark the loops that have two sets of wires so that no attempt is made to attach peaks or a square at these points.)

Make the first loop of beads D-1, E-1, E-2, and F-1 in the middle of a 9 foot length of #30 wire, A. This loop is shown on Figure 31 above.

Center a 3 x 6 mm bead (D-2) on a second 9 foot piece of wire, B. String one end of B through the E-2 bead already woven on wire A. String a 6 mm bead (E-3) on the other end of wire B. Cross over both ends of B in another 3 x 6 mm bead, F-2. See Figure 32 above.

Center a 3 x 6 mm bead (D-3) on a third 9 foot wire, C. Run one end of C through the previously woven E-3 bead on wire B and the other end of wire C through the already woven E-1 bead on wire A. See Figure 33 on page 25. Cross over the C wire ends in another 3 x 6 mm bead, F-3. This is the first complete loop of the triangular base of the circle. Continue the weave as it was begun. Notice that the weave has a hollow core at its center. Place the 6 mm rounds on the lengthwise wires; see beads E and G. Use the 3 x 6 ovals (F) on the crossovers. The weave must be tight; the hollow triangular tube must have exactly 87 sets of three 6 mm lengthwise and 88 sets of three 3 x 6 mm crossovers when the first beads are included in the count. Do NOT cut off the excess wires.

If two sets of 5 foot wires each were used, the piecing loops begin on the 45th set of 3 x 6 mm ovals. Slight differences in bead size may require more or fewer loops to make a circle of no less than 8 inches inside diameter. If so, change the number of beads to what is needed. But the number of crossover sets must be divisible by four to center the square border.

Lay the tube straight on a flat surface. Work a 36 inch straight piece of #14 green florist wire into and through the length of the triangular tube. Push the wire with one hand while steadying the tube on the surface with the other hand. Another person may hold the tube with both hands while the wire is pushed with two hands. The green wire should extend several inches beyond each end of the tube. Keep one side of the triangle on the flat surface while the bead covered green wire is curved to a circle of 8 inches inside diameter. Cut off exactly 9 inches of the #14 green wire.

Close the weave of the triangular tube by adding a set of three 6 mm rounds to the leftover #30 wires to complete the 88th loop. Adjust the weave on the green wire so that the weave fits the wire exactly. Then weave the leftover wires into the first woven D, E, and F beads. Some wires may be carried into the G beads to anchor them further. Cut off the excess wire. Mark the loops where the wires in the tubular weave are double by running safety pins through those loops. When positioning the peaks, rays, and squares on the circles, place them where the weaving wires are NOT double.

* * *

PEAKS & RAYS for the Person & Trinity Circles:

Figure 34 on this page shows the position of the peaks and rays on slightly more than a quarter of the circle. Figure 35, also on this page, shows the wiring for an individual ray. Figure 36 on page 28 diagrams the size and number of beads on one-fourth of the circle. (If the number of circle beads changes, the spacing, position, and/or number of the peaks and rays must be rearranged for a balanced effect.)

Loop the middle of a 15 inch length of #30 wire around the wires that lead into the outside oval circle bead where it connects (A on Figure 35) with the top 6 mm round. String the proper number and size beads over both ends of the wire. For the shortest ray, the front (C) is a 6 mm, a 5 mm, two 4 mm, and a 3 mm bead. Then run one wire only through another 3 mm bead. Continue both wires through one 3 mm, two 4 mm, a 5 mm, and a 6 mm bead for the back of the ray, B. Pull both wires tight. Run one wire through the outside top oval; run the other wire through the bottom oval from outside to inside the circle, through the inside oval (IS) and on up through the front of the ray, C. Pull the wires tight; cut off the excess wire. Curve the ray to the flame shape shown on Figure 34.

To start a peak, run a 15 inch length of #30 wire through the top 6 mm round circle bead that the peak straddles; see A on Figure 36. Center the bead on the wire. Run two 6 mm, a 5 mm, a 4 mm, and a 3 mm bead over each wire in that order. Then run both wires through a 5 mm, a 4 mm, and two 3 mm beads. Run both

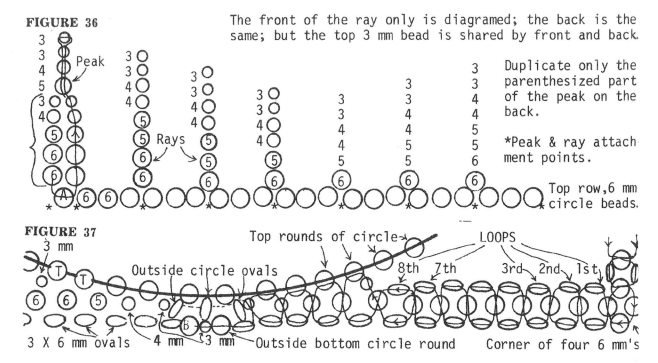

FIGURE 36 — The front of the ray only is diagramed; the back is the same; but the top 3 mm bead is shared by front and back.

Duplicate only the parenthesized part of the peak on the back.

*Peak & ray attachment points.

Top row, 6 mm circle beads.

FIGURE 37

wires back through the first strung 3 mm bead, the 4 mm, and the 5 mm beads. Pull the wires tight. String a 3 mm, a 4 mm, a 5 mm, and two 6 mm beads on each wire. Run each wire from the outside to the inside of the circle through a bottom oval at the side of the starting round—one wire through the oval on one side, the other on the opposite side. Continue each wire up through its corresponding inside oval and front leg of the peak. Pull the wires tight and cut off the leftovers.

SQUARES for the Season Symbols:

The square is a straight weave of 6 mm cross over beads and 3 x 6 mm lengthwise ovals except at the corners (which are four 6 mm beads) and the four places where the square weaves into the circle. Each side of the square has the four 6 mm corner, eight loops of rounds and ovals, nine loops that weave into the circle (which involve ten circle loops), eight loops of rounds and ovals, and the corner loop.

Figure 37 on this page diagrams the weave from the right corner to the left and through the circle. Begin by centering a 6 mm bead on a 5 foot length of #30 wire. Weave seven loops of 6 mm's on the crossovers and 3 x 6 mm ovals on the lengthwise wires. Then weave the 6 mm corner loop of four 6 mm rounds as shown at A; next weave eight loops of ovals and rounds.

On the weave through the circle, the square's inner edge becomes the top row of the circle's 6 mm beads; the square's crossover beads become smaller as the circle absorbs the square; then the square dips to the bottom of the circle as the outer edges of the circle and the square coincide. This process, which is diagramed on Figure 37, is explained bead by bead:

Cross over the wires in the 6 mm bead at the end of the 8th loop. Right wire through a 3 mm bead and through a top 6 mm bead of the circle; left wire through a 3 x 6 mm; cross over both wires in a 6 mm bead. Right wire through the next top circle bead; left wire through a 3 x 6 mm bead; cross over both wires in a 5 mm. Right wire through the next top circle bead; left wire through a 3 x 6 mm; cross over in a 4 mm. Right wire through the next top bead; left wire through a 3 x 6 mm; cross over the wires in a 3 mm. Right wire into the core of the weave behind the next three ovals; left wire through a 3 x 6 mm oval; left wire through the next outside bottom circle bead, B; left wire through a 3 mm bead. This 3 mm bead is the middle and bottom of one side of the square. From this point, the square rises to the top of the circle and moves to its outer edge and away from it. Weave out of the circle by reversing the procedure into it. Continue the square weave around the circle until the four sides are complete.

If the circle has 88 loops, twelve 6 mm beads will be between each point at which the square joins the circle. Piece the weaving wires at the corners away from the circle.

PRESENT HALF-SIZE BORDERS

Use metal beads only. For a close-up view of the half-size present Person border, see the Hand on page 31, right. A similar view of a matching Season border is around the Rose on page 32.

Materials: 20 gauge copper color wire; #30 gold hair wire; 3, 4, 5, 6, 8, and 3 x 6 mm gold metal beads; gold rocailles.

BORDERS

FIGURE 38 o-Rocailles   ⬭-3 X 6 mm's
O -3 mm's

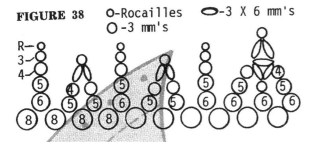

FIGURE 39

One side of square

Weave around gap between circle beads
Circle of 8 mm beads

DIRECTIONS

Both the season and Person circles are forty 8 mm beads on 20 gauge wire. Construction of the circle begins, like that of the original, by bending a triangle at one end of a length of the wire. Shape the wire to a 4 1/8 inch circle.

* * *

Figure 38 above diagrams one-fourth of the Person circle's weave. Twist the end of a piece of #30 wire around the triangle in the circle wire to hold. Run an 8 mm bead over both wires; push the bead against the triangle. To make ray A, string beads on the #30 wire only in this order: a 6 mm, a 5 mm, a 4 mm, a 3 mm, and a gold rocaille. Run the wire back through the metal beads only in reverse order. Pull the wires tight. Run an 8 mm bead over both the #30 and 20 gauge wires; push the bead tight against the first 8 mm bead. String an 8 mm bead on the 20 gauge wire only.

For peak B, string a 5 mm, a 4 mm, a 3 x 6 mm, a 3 mm, a 3 x 6 mm, a 4 mm, and a 5 mm bead on the #30 wire. Run an 8 mm bead over both wires. Turn the top 3 mm bead on the peak so that the #30 wires cross over themselves to make the top ends of the 3 x 6 mm beads touch. Run an 8 mm bead over the #30 and the 20 gauge wires. Continue to bead the circle and its extensions to the beginning of peak C.

To bead peak C, run the #30 wire through a 6 mm, a 5 mm, a 4 mm, a 3 x 6 mm, a 3 mm, and two 3 x 6 mm beads. Then, again run the wire up through the first 3 x 6 mm and down through the second 3 x 6 mm. Tighten the wires to close the D triangle. String a 3 x 6 mm, a 3 mm, and a 6 mm on the #30 wire. String an 8 mm bead on the 20 gauge circle wire. Then loop the #30 wire around the 20 gauge circle wire and next to the 8 mm bead on that wire. Run the #30 wire back through the 6 mm and the 3 mm beads. Run another 3 x 6 mm over the wire; pull the wire tight and run it through the horizontal 3 x 6 mm to close triangle E. String a 4 mm, a 5 mm, and a 6 mm on the wire to complete the right leg of the peak to the circle wire. Run an 8 mm over the circle wire only.

This is one-fourth of the border. Repeat the design around the circle. At the end, bend a triangle in the 20 gauge wire to match the first triangle. Twist #30 wire around the triangles to hold them together.

* * *

This season border is basically a straight weave of 3 x 6 mm gold metal beads. Each corner is a square of 3 x 6 mm ovals, which is drawn as a square on Detail 1 of Figure 39 on this page. Note on Detail 2 that squares which are side by side share a common crossover. Each side of the square border consists of one 3 x 6 mm corner square, two 3 mm beads, thirteen 3 x 6 mm squares, two 3 mm beads, and the corner square.

Begin the weave on two pieces of #30 wire at A on Detail 3. Handle the two wires as one. Make a straight weave of 3 x 6 mm ovals on the lengthwise and crossover wires. At B, run a 3 mm bead on each pair of lengthwise wires. Cross over the wires in a 3 x 6 mm. String two 3 x 6 mm ovals on one pair of wires; cross over both pairs of wires in another 3 x 6 mm bead to turn the corner. Run a 3 mm bead on each pair of wires. Continue the straight weave of 3 x 6 mm ovals to the corner. Turn the corner. Continue the weave around the border until it is complete. Anchor the wires by running them through two loops at the start of the weave.

String ten 8 mm beads on a shaped 20 gauge wire circle. Push them against the triangular end. Run the 20 gauge circle wire through the middle square on one side of the square border. String ten more 8 mm beads on the circle wire; run the 20 gauge wire through the middle square on the next side of the square. Continue to string beads and to lace the circle wire through the sides of the square until each side is joined. The square undulates over and under the circle which is flat.

SIMPLIFIED PRESENT BORDERS

Simplified season borders may be made by shaping stranded wire to a circle and a square, which just touches the circle at four points. Wrap each with 1½ inch vinyl festooning. Join the two together at the points where they touch with #30 wire wrapped from the circle to the square in a figure 8.

Or light coat hanger wires may be shaped to a circle and a square. String each with 10 mm gold glass beads. Wire them together at the four points where they touch by twisting #30 wire in a figure 8 between the two figures.

SEASON & PERSON SYMBOLS

The chief difference between Chrismons of the Basic Series and the Christian Year Series is that those in the latter group are either animate beings or inanimate objects rather than letters, monograms, and/or geometric figures. Because these concrete symbols are well known, one may be tempted to be too realistic. Remember what the goal really is! One is not, for example, trying to model a perfect phoenix; one is trying to give a sense of the shock and triumph, the joy and glory of the Resurrection!

While the bird that is made must be recognizable so that the reference is understood, it is not necessary to show every feather to convey the idea of victory. That is not to say that one may work carelessly. All through this Series the Chrismon maker is talking about God. If that God is really the worker's God, the worker will want his or her words (in this case, the words are the handiwork) to be the best of which he or she is capable. But perfection is God's attribute, not man's. What we do here is for His glory, not ours.

* * *

A comparison of the back cover photograph of the present Christian Year Series with the front cover picture of the simplified Series shows that symbols are simplified, in the main, by eliminating beadwork. Chrismons which were originally white beadwork become glittered styrofoam; gold beading becomes foil. Glitter and foil are less expensive and easier to work than beads.

Complete directions for executing all the season and Person symbols by the simplified methods are given. White beaded Chrismons become carved styrofoam to which white iris glitter is applied. The star, shamrock, dove, lamb, hand, and pelican are treated in this manner. To learn how to follow the patterns and to build up skill in this procedure, construct the carved symbols in the order that they are listed above.

The gold-beaded flames become gold foil; the gold-beaded sides of the chariot, gold-backed paper. Since the remainder of the original symbols — the scroll, the gladiolus or rose, and the butterfly — are relatively easy to make, they were not simplified; the original and simplified designs are the same. Anyone who has made Chrismons in the "somewhat difficult" category in the Basic Series can easily construct the entire simplified Christian Year Series.

* * *

The Christian Year season and Person symbols become more difficult when they are made by the original beaded procedures. Such methods are: 1) Straight line weave (phoenix-inner wing, triangle); 2) Single line wired beads (phoenix-tail, lamb-leg); 3) Bead mosaic (phoenix, dove-bodies); 4) Strung bead mosaic (phoenix-head, pelican-body); 5) Parallel bugle weave (flames, pelican-wing tips). To follow the original methods, make the phoenix first. Complete directions are given for this symbol only. Since this one design covers so many procedures, what is learned on the phoenix can be adapted to the other symbols.

Complete directions for the remainder of the original designs (unless they are like the simplified) are not given because no one could follow them. Even the writer cannot duplicate the original Series; the original materials — pearls in odd tints and shapes — could never be reassembled. No purpose is served in giving instructions for which the supplies cannot be found.

On the other hand, it is possible to approximate the effect of the original designs. Under the directions for each symbol, the original methods are outlined. After reading those suggestions, examine the picture of the ornament. Then from the materials that can be obtained, develop a design that gives the desired effect. Apply the experience gained in the construction of the phoenix to working out and making the other symbols. Thus, one creates his or her own original Series.

While many groups prefer not to invest this much work in the project, others do want the challenge and joy of accomplishment that such an undertaking offers. Some succeed in doing a better job than was originally done. Once for a display, Ascension Church borrowed the hand from Good Shepherd Church in Mt. Holly, North Carolina, because it was better than the original one. Your group may desire to do similar work.

SEASON & PERSON SYMBOLS

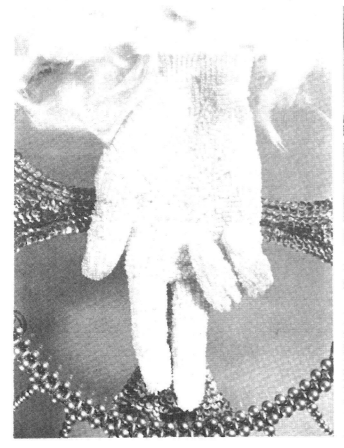

SEASON & PERSON SYMBOLS

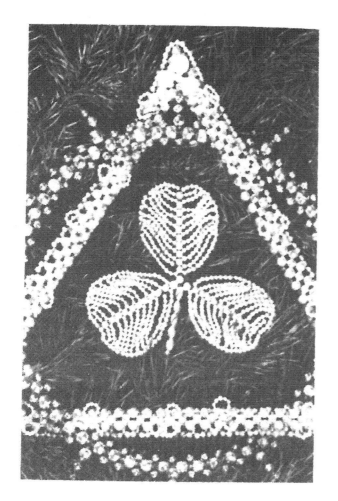

32

SEASON & PERSON SYMBOLS

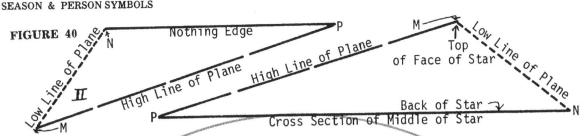

FIGURE 40

GENERAL DIRECTIONS FOR STYROFOAM SYMBOLS

Pattern Lines:

Since shapes like the five-point star are common, directions for carved Chrismons begin with this symbol. This familiar shape should help to clarify the pattern lines' meaning. These same lines are on all the carved patterns. If their meaning is learned on the star, that information may be used to interpret less known designs. The colored background on this page is the pattern to which the following directions refer.

On its back, the star is flat. The front is composed of ten flat planes or surfaces, which are numbered clockwise with Roman numerals. M, in the middle, is the highest point; it is one inch thick. P and N, on the edges, feather off into nothingness along the PN solid line around the edge of the star.

The long dashed lines MP indicate the high line of the ten planes; MN, the dotted lines, represent the low lines of each plane. Detail 1 of Figure 40, above, shows one plane, MNP. Compare this with plane II in the background figure. Detail 2 is a cross-section through the middle.

Another kind of line, a solid line along the edge of the pattern with V's drawn inside it, is not shown on the star pattern. A solid line with zigzags next to it indicates an edge line that is not carried into nothingness. The cross-section of the shamrock (Figure 42 on page 35) shows the thickness of a zigzagged line. The pattern's solid line is the finished edge.

Finishes for Styrofoam:

Styrofoam symbols may have either a glittered (rough) or pearlized (smooth) finish. Compare the glittered star (upper left) on page 31 with the pearlized hand at the upper right of page 31.

Applying glitter adds about 1/16 inch thickness to foam. If a design is to be glittered, the carved symbol must be a little smaller than the desired finished Chrismon. To glitter styrofoam, paint the surface with water thinned glue (2/3 white glue, 1/3 water). Immediately sprinkle the wet surface with white iris glitter. Lay the ornament on waxed paper to dry.

If the styrofoam is to have a smooth coating, the carved foam must be a bit larger than the finished design. Pearlizing directions are in "Finishing the Styrofoam" in the General Directions for wedding symbols in *Chrismons for Every Day* and under the hand on page 37.

THE RAYED NIMBUS

For centuries, Christian artists have used the triradiant nimbus, a circle of light with three rays of light from the center, to designate God. Some artists use four rays to form a cross, which is called a cruciform nimbus. The rayed nimbus always denotes divinity; it is used only on a subject meant to depict or symbolize God or a Person of the Triune.

The nimbi on Figure 41 below are for the Descending Dove. It is the only detailed drawing of the nimbus that is given. On other figures, enough of the nimbus is shown to indicate the outside diameter from which a pattern can be made. Personal preference determines whether the rays are curved or straight.

Original Chrismon: Spray ordinary metal window screening gold. Cut a circle of the screening to the outside diameter of the nimbus. Sew 5 mm gold sequins-by-the-yard to the screening to make the three rays and circles as shown on the left drawing. Sequins may be sewn to make the straight-line as well as the curved nimbus.

Simplified Chrismon: Cut the circle and rays, in one piece, from gold sequin material, gold foil, or two pieces of gold-backed paper glued together. Curved or straight rays may be made.

Original or Simplified: Pin and glue the nimbus, through the crucial point, to the back of the head as shown on the patterns. If necessary, also pin through one or more of the rays. The rayed nimbus is generally placed so that the crucial point is behind the eyes.

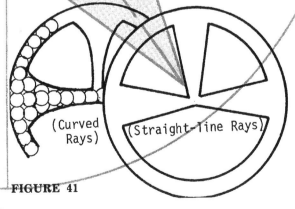

(Curved Rays) (Straight-line Rays)

FIGURE 41

EPIPHANY STAR (Five-Point Star)

Photographs: Original, lower right of page 31; Simplified & Half-Size, upper left of page 31; Present, page 32.

SIMPLIFIED DESIGN

Materials: 1″ thick white styrofoam; 10 mm, 4 x 8 mm, and seed pearls; white pipe cleaners; #30 hair wire; styrofoam glue; white, white iris, or crystal glitter.

Directions:

Cut the star from one inch thick styrofoam by the solid outer line of the pattern which is the colored background of page 33. With an X-acto type knife or a serrated paring knife, carve the ten planes to make the dimensional star.

Make five pipe cleaner hangers on which three ten inch lengths of #30 wire extend from the bend in the cleaner. (See "Hangers" in the general information in the *Basic Series*. Twist the three wires together for one-fourth inch from the bend in the cleaner. Insert and glue the pipe cleaner's ends into the back of the star so that the wires come out from behind a corner of the star like the rays on the pattern.

Apply white iris glitter to the back of the star. Let it dry. On the front of the star, push a 10 mm pearl into the center peak at M to make a depression in the foam; make depressions on the top of the MP peak lines for a row of 4 x 8 mm pearls as shown on the pattern. Apply glitter to the front of the star except in the depressions where the pearls are to be set. Then glue the pearls in place. Three mm pearls may be pinned and glued along the outer edges. (If desired, the pearls may be omitted.)

Set the star in its border by the ray wires. First string the approximate number of needed seed pearls on the center wire of each set of three rays. Center the star in the circle; attach each wire at its proper space between the beads on the wire frame. Add or remove beads to hold the star at the center of the circle without sagging. Twist the wires around the frame wire to hold; cut off the excess #30 wire. String seed beads on each of the other wires; attach them to the circle wire at the next bead space on either side of the middle ray.

ORIGINAL DESIGN

Materials: 1″ thick white styrofoam; 8 mm, 4 mm, 3 mm, 3 x 6 mm, and seed pearls; white thread; #30 hair wire; white painted metal window screening; styrofoam glue.

Directions:

This design is made by the strung bead mosaic method. See the Jerusalem Cross in the *Basic Series* for specific instructions on how to set the pearls, which are strung on white thread, on to the styrofoam.

Carve the star from one inch styrofoam like the simplified star above. Insert and glue the three-wire hangers as described above. Cut a star one-half inch larger than the pattern from white-painted screening. Fold the edges under so that the screening star is the same size as the back of the styrofoam star. Glue the screening to the back of the styrofoam star.

Push the 8 mm pearl into the center top of the star; glue it in place. Glue a string of 4 mm pearls to the top front of each peak from P to M. Glue 3 x 6 mm pearls around the edge of the star and on the MN lines between the peaks. Cover the remaining front surfaces of the star with 3 mm pearls strung on thread.

Cover the back of the star with white iris glitter. String seed pearls on the ray wires; attach the star to the border by those wires.

PRESENT DESIGN

Materials: Crystal cooking crystals; setting liquid; #30 hair wire; transparent and white satin bugle beads; stiff aluminum foil.

Directions:

Make the star by the directions for the five-point star on the God-Man wreath on page 49 in *Chrismons for Every Day* except for these changes:
1) Make the paper pattern one-fourth inch larger around the edge of the star.
2) Move the X points one-half inch closer to the pattern edge.
3) To make the "spider," substitute three #30 wires for each #20 wire in the original spider. Twist the three wires together to the point where they emerge from the foil to become the three rays as on the simplified design above.

Set the star into the border by the rays as directed under the simplified design. String the center ray of each trio with white satin bugles, the outer rays with transparent bugles.

HALF-SIZE DESIGNS

Materials: 1″ thick white styrofoam; white pipe cleaners; #30 hair wire; white glue; white iris glitter; 5 mm, 3 x 6 mm, and seed pearls.

Directions:

The colored star on the background of this page is the pattern for the half-size star. The carving lines are the same as on the full-size star. Construct the star by the simplified directions with the following exceptions:
1) Use a 5 mm pearl at the center top; use 3 x 6 mm oval pearls along the MP peak lines.
2) Hang the star in the border by only one ray from each inside corner of the star.

Or the half-size star may be made like the present star by using the background pattern as the paper pattern. Use only one ray from each corner of the star. Move the X marks one-fourth inch toward the center of the foil pattern.

SEASON & PERSON SYMBOLS

SHAMROCK IN TRIANGLE INTERWOVEN WITH CIRCLE

Photographs: Original, upper left of page 32; Simplified & Half-Size, lower right of page 32.

SIMPLIFIED SHAMROCK (Full & Half-Size)

Materials: ½" white styrofoam; white iris glitter; styrofoam glue; pipe cleaner hangers; 3 x 6 mm pearls; 10 mm or 5 mm pearl.

Directions:

Cut out the full-size shamrock from one-half inch styrofoam by the colored background pattern on page 30. (Cut the half-size by the colored pattern on the same page.) Carve the foam by the pattern lines. Note that the zigzag line at its D points is the thickest part of the shamrock's cross section on Figure 42 below. The flat stem is as deep as its width.

FIGURE 42

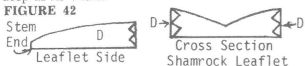

To carve a star in planes that form high and low V's is natural. But one may prefer to round off the foam in natural designs. A contemporary look results when angular cuts are retained. (We prefer it.) However, if a natural appearance is wanted, round off the carvings.

Make a depression where the leaves and stem meet for a 10 mm pearl (a 5 mm pearl in the half-size). Attach a pipe cleaner hanger at points E on the outer back of each leaflet. Cover the back, sides, and front (except at the depression) with white glitter. Glue the center pearl in place. If wanted, glue a row of 3 x 6 mm pearls along the center line of each leaflet.

ORIGINAL & PRESENT SHAMROCK

Materials: 3 mm, 5 mm, and 4 x 8 mm pearls; #30 hair wire.

Directions:

Wrap a piece of pipe cleaner around a 6 foot length of #30 wire. Run both ends of the wire through ten 5 mm pearls, A to K on Figure 43 on this page. Anchor the wires so that one is five feet long. Run the short wire from K through another 5 mm pearl, L; carry the short wire back around and through bead L to anchor it.

Run the long wire from K around and through K again to anchor it. String 27 three mm pearls on that wire. Take the pipe cleaner off the #30 wire; continue the wire through the loop of the #30 wire above A. String 27 more 3 mm pearls on the wire; run the wire up through K. Pull the wire tight; anchor it. Shape the 3 mm pearls to the leaf outline. The 5 mm midrib pearls are loose because of the play left in the wires when the pipe cleaner was removed.

To weave the leaf, string ten 3 mm pearls on the wire from K. See Figure 44 on this page.

Run the wire up through the 13th and 14th right edge beads from K; tighten the wire. String 10 more 3 mm pearls. Run the wire down through bead J; tighten the wire; anchor it. String 10 more 3 mm pearls; run the wire up through the 13th and 14th beads on the left edge. String 10 more 3 mm beads; run the wire up through bead H. Two veins are now on each side of the leaf.

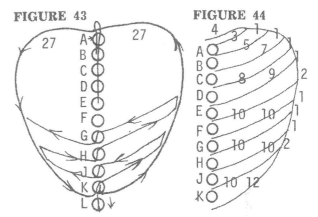

Continue to weave veins up the leaf; alternate from one side to the other. Figure 44 shows the number of beads in each vein and the number to run through or skip between veins. After the last vein on the left, push the beads tight; wrap the wire twice around the wire loop above A. This wire becomes a hanger. Make three leaflets like this.

Run the wires from the three L beads through five 4 x 8 mm stem pearls. Run two wires only through a 3 mm pearl and back through the stem pearls. Tighten the wires; cut off their excess. The wire left at the 3 mm bead is the hanger.

FULL-SIZE PRESENT & SIMPLIFIED TRIANGLE

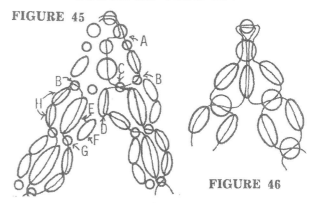

Because the weave of the present triangle is superior to that of the original, directions for the latter are not given.

Materials: 3 mm, 4 mm, 8 mm, 5 x 7 mm, and 8 x 14 mm pearls; #30 hair wire.

SEASON & PERSON SYMBOLS

Directions:

Begin the weave at the top of Figure 45 on page 35. Run three 4 mm pearls on two 24 inch pieces of #30 wire. Put the ends of one wire together; run a 4 mm and an 8 mm pearl on the wires; push the pearls against the first pearls; anchor the wires. On each of the other wires at A, string a 3 mm, a 5 x 7 mm, and a 3 mm pearl, B. Cross over one of these wires with a wire from the 8 mm pearl in another 3 mm pearl, C.

The left side of Figure 45 shows the insertion of an extra 24 inch #30 wire into each leg. Center the wire on bead B; run the two center wires from beads C through a 5 x 7 oval, D; anchor the wires. Run the other wire from C with one end of the inserted wire through an 8 x 14 mm pearl, E; anchor. Run one wire from D through a 5 x 7 mm F; cross over that wire with one from E in a 3 mm G. Run the other end of the inserted wire at C through two 5 x 7 mm's H; cross over that wire with the remaining wire from E in a 3 mm pearl. Continue to weave each leg on four wires until the leg has nine 8 x 14 mm beads. The center 8 x 14 mm lengthwise beads each carry two wires; the edge lengthwise beads are a pair of 5 x 7 mm pearls on one wire.

Weave the other two corners. Place the three corners so that they form a triangle with eighteen 8 x 14 mm pearls in each side. Join the sides by crossing over the wires from both ends in the middle 3 mm pearls. Weave the wires for another loop to anchor them. Cut off the excess.

Before joining the last side of the triangle, interweave the triangle with the circle as shown on the photographs. The circle is flat while the triangle undulates over and under it. Wire the two together where they touch. Suspend the shamrock in the center by its hanging wires.

HALF-SIZE TRIANGLE

Weave the triangle of 5 mm and 5 x 7 mm pearls except for each corner pearl which is a 3 mm pearl. Start the weave at a corner with a 3 mm pearl centered on two lengths of #30 wire. Follow the weaving diagram on Figure 46 on page 35. Weave half the leg from each corner.

Join the legs as explained in the directions for the present triangle. Each leg in the half-size triangle has 17 five mm crossovers; the lengthwise beads are 5 x 7 mm pearls.

OPTIONAL SHELL SHAMROCKS

A shell shamrock may be attached to the front of each corner of the triangle. To make a shamrock, use 5 mm half round pearls with settings and 10 mm white iris shell sequins. Place a setting on a flat surface. Put the holes of three shells over three prongs of the setting. Lay a ten inch length of #30 wire across the center of the setting. Place the half round pearl on top; tighten the prongs of the setting against the pearl. The wired shamrock is ready to attach.

DESCENDING DOVE

Photograph: Original & Present, page 26.

SIMPLIFIED DOVE

Materials: 1" white styrofoam; styrofoam glue; white iris glitter; gold sequin material or gold-backed paper; gold rocailles; #30 hair wire; white pipe cleaners.

Directions:

Cut the dove out of one inch styrofoam by the solid outline of the colored background of this page. Carve the styrofoam to look like the back of the bird. (The dove's back is most often shown when it symbolizes the Holy Spirit.) Figure 47 below, a cross section of the dove, shows the relative proportions to work for.

Cover the entire dove with white, white iris, or crystal glitter. Cut the nimbus from gold sequin material or gold-backed paper glued to heavy paper. Pin and glue it in place.

FIGURE 47 Cross Section of the Dove
Head   Body   Tail

Make a pipe cleaner hanger with seven six inch strands of #30 wire. (Twist the middle of three 12 inch pieces and the end of a 7 inch piece on the pipe cleaner.) With a compass point, push two holes through the nimbus ray into the underside of the beak. Glue the hanger in place. Insert and glue an ordinary hanger on each side of the tail back.

Suspend the dove in its circle by the two tail hangers so that the tail is 3/8 to 1/2 inch below the circle. Bead the middle wire under the dove's beak with gold rocailles to reach from the nimbus to the circle. Attach the wire to the circle to hold the dove tautly in place. Bead the six other wires in like manner. Space them on and attach them to the circle as shown on the pattern.

HALF-SIZE DOVE

The home-size dove is made like the simplified symbol except that it is cut from one-half inch styrofoam. In addition, the beaded rays from the head are not used. Instead attach the bottom of the dove to the circle with an ordinary foam hanger into the head. The half-size pattern is on the colored background of page 34.

SEASON & PERSON SYMBOLS

ORIGINAL & PRESENT DOVE

The dove is made by the bead mosaic method; the styrofoam bed is from ¼ to ⅛ inch thick. Pearls from 4 x 8 mm to 12 x 20 mm are used. The wing and tail tips are seed pearls; blank spaces are set with 3 x 6 mm, 3 mm, 4 mm, and 5 mm pearls. The lines of baroque pearls with their seed pearl tips are strung on #30 wire before they are glued to the foam and sewn (through the foam) to the screening back.

Glue and/or sew gold sequins-by-the-yard to outline the gold screening nimbus and its rays. For the water, alternate crystal love beads with eight 8 mm cut crystal beads on #20 silver color wire. Bend the wire to a zigzag line.

Make a ray by twisting a piece of #30 wire to hold in a hole at the edge of the nimbus. Bead the wire with gold rocailles to the water line. Then loop the wire around the #20 silver wire. Finally fasten the wire to the circle. Place seven rays from the nimbus to the water.

HAND FROM CLOUD

Photographs: Original & Present, lower left of page 31; Simplified & Half-Size, upper right of page 31.

SIMPLIFIED & HALF-SIZE HAND

Materials: 1" or ½" white styrofoam; styrofoam glue; white spray paint; pearlized spray finish; gold sequin material; glass wool or other cloud-like material; styrofoam hangers.

Directions:

Cut the full-size hand out of one inch styrofoam by the colored background pattern on page 29. Use one-half inch foam for the half-size pattern on the background of page 34. Carve the design by the pattern lines. Make the hand and fingers thick enough; if it is too thin, the symbol looks like a glove rather than a hand.

Cover the entire surface with a thick coat of white glue; let it dry. While smoothing a knife blade over the hand's surface, apply pressure to even out the rough surfaces. Apply another coat of glue; let it dry. Again smooth the surface. After another coat of glue, sand irregularities away. Apply another coat of glue. Spray paint the surface white; then apply a coat of pearlized finish. (If desired, the surface may be finished with white iris glitter for a rough rather than a smooth appearance.)

Cut out the rays, either curved or straight, from gold-backed paper glued to light cardboard or gold sequin material. Make a complete pattern for the rays by continuing their lines until they meet under the hand. When they are made of gold-backed paper, cut the three rays in one piece. But sequin material rays must be cut in two pieces: One makes the two side rays; the bottom ray is cut from another piece of material. (When the rays are fastened to the hand, pin through both layers into the hand.)

Reinforce the ends of each ray by sticking two layers of transparent plastic tape to the back of the last one-half inch of each ray as indicated at B. With a compass point or a strong needle, punch holes along the edge of each ray as marked on the pattern.

Glue and pin the rays to the back of the hand. Glue styrofoam hangers, one for each ray, into the back of the hand. Place one behind the thumb, another in the middle of the palm, and the other behind the third finger tip. Attach two hangers in the wrist as shown at D.

Lay the hand, palm down, on the beaded circle; match the ray edges to the border circle. Carry the hanger wires behind each ray to its edge; fasten them to hold tautly around the circle wires. Attach the wrist hangers in the same way. Loop gold thread around the circle wires and through the punched holes in the ray ends to hold the rays smoothly to the circle.

For the cloud, use either glass wool (available at pet shops for filtering aquarium water) or angel hair (a Christmas decoration). Both are spun glass which has a soft, cloud-like appearance. Handle it carefully; it cuts. Drape the wool around the wrist to look like a cloud. Stitches at the wrist and looped around the circle will hold the cloud in place.

ORIGINAL & PRESENT HAND

Materials: 1" white styrofoam; gold & white screening; styrofoam hangers; white & gold thread; white seed pearls; white glue; 5 mm sequins-by-the-yard; #30 wire; glass wool.

Directions:

The hand is made by the strung-bead mosaic method. Carve a hand from one inch styrofoam as directed for the simplified Chrismon but leave the back surface flat. From white screening, cut a hand one-half inch larger than the pattern. Fold the edges of the screening under to make a hand one-eighth inch smaller than the pattern. Fasten it to the back of the carved hand with U-shaped pieces of pipe cleaner.

Lay lines of seed pearls strung on white thread over the front and sides of the hand. Sew (through the styrofoam and over a line of the screening) and glue the strung pearls in place. Careful placement of the pearls can show the lines of the hand and fingers.

From gold wire screening, cut the rays a half-inch larger than the pattern. Fold the edges under to make the rays an eighth inch smaller than the pattern. Sew 5 mm gold sequins-by-the-yard to cover the screen. Cover the screen back of the hand with white iris glitter.

Follow the simplified directions to join the hand, the rays, and the cloud.

SEASON & PERSON SYMBOLS

SEASON & PERSON SYMBOLS

LAMB WITH BANNER OF VICTORY

Photographs: Original & Present, above; the wreath and miniature lambs on the back cover of *Chrismons for Every Day* are made in the same manner and proportions as the Simplified & Half-Size Lambs.

SIMPLIFIED FULL-SIZE LAMB

Materials: 1" white styrofoam; crystal glitter; white glue; gold sequin material; gold-backed paper; rocaille, 6 mm, & 3 x 6 mm gold beads; beading wire; #30 wire; #18 green florist wire; white thread; pipe cleaner hangers.

Directions:

Cut the lamb from one inch styrofoam by the outline on the colored background pattern on this page. Carve it by the pattern lines.

Cut the banner from ¼ inch styrofoam; press the foam to flatten it to ⅛ inch. Paint it with white glue to strengthen it. Cut the cross from gold-backed paper; glue it to the banner.

For the banner staff, make a tiny loop at one end of an 8 inch piece of #18 green florist wire. Twist an 18 inch piece of beading wire to hold around the loop so that one end of the wire is 4 inches long. Run a 3 x 6 mm gold bead over the florist wire and the 14 inch beading wire end. String a 3 x 6 mm bead and a gold rocaille over the beading wire only; run the wire back through the 3 x 6 mm bead; tighten the wire to make the bead stand out. Make the other arm of the cross on the beading wire with another 3 x 6 mm and rocaille bead. Then string 4 x 6 mm ovals over both wires to complete the staff. Twist a tiny loop in the #18 wire to hold the beads in place. The beading wire ends become hanger wires to fasten the lamb in its circle. Sew the banner to the staff by looping thread around the beads and through the edge of the banner.

Carve out the lamb's back to allow the staff to run in front of the right foot and nimbus and behind the body. Press a 6 mm gold bead in the eye position. Cover the lamb (except the banner cutout and eye hole) with white iris glitter. Glue the eye in place; pin and glue the banner staff with U-shaped pipe cleaner pieces.

Cut the nimbus from gold sequin material. Pin and glue it in place. Insert and glue a styrofoam hanger into the back of the head and another into the tail. Suspend the lamb in the middle of its circle with the hanger wires and the wires from the staff. A red bead may be glued at the throat for the sacrificial wound.

HALF-SIZE LAMB

Carve the home-size lamb from one inch styrofoam by the colored background pattern on page 34. The nimbus and banner patterns are also on that page. Make it like the simplified lamb but use a 4 mm gold bead for the eye.

ORIGINAL & PRESENT LAMB

Make the body, head, and neck of the lamb by the bead mosaic method. Use the head and body of the simplified pattern as a guide for the styrofoam bed which is one eighth to one half inch thick. Back it with white screening.

The neck and body are alternate rows of 3 mm and 4 mm pearls and 8 mm pearls tipped with 2 mm pearls. Before laying the rows on the bed, they are strung on #30 wire which is hooked into the screen backing. The pearls in the row along the bottom of the body are 10 mm.

The head is of 3 mm and 4 mm pearls strung on thread before they are sewn (through the foam) to the screen backing. Make the eye by sewing a 6 mm gold bead in place. An 8 x 16 mm oblong pearl is pinned and glued in place for the ear.

Assorted round, oval, and oblong pearls from 8 mm to 8 x 16 mm in size make up the legs. String the end pearl in the middle of the wire for the foot; then run both wire ends through the leg pearls. Fasten them to the screening back with the leftover wires at top. Five mm gold sequins-by-the-yard outline the gold screening nimbus and its rays.

The banner is made like the simplified design with these exceptions:
1) The banner pattern at the upper right is carved in three dimensions. Seed pearls are glued in a line at the center of the cross.
2) Bead the #18 staff wire to the point at which it touches the lamb's shoulder. Then lace it to the screening until it emerges at the leg where it is again beaded to its end.

On the present lamb only, the banner is of pearl seed and gold rocaille beads. The beading style is that of Indian belts and rings.

SEASON & PERSON SYMBOLS

PHOENIX RISING FROM THE FLAMES

Photograph: Original & Present, page 38.

SIMPLIFIED & HOME-SIZE PHOENIX

There are three birds in the original Christian Year Series. Because they are in a variety of bead types, shapes, and shades, each appears quite different from the others. When the Series is made by the simplified method however, every bird is made of glitter-covered, carved styrofoam. As a result, the birds may appear similar.

This situation can be relieved by using the butterfly for the Easter symbol. (Note the comments on "Easter" on page 7.) Actually, a butterfly (or a lily) balances the gladiolus or rose for Christmas better than the phoenix. Except for the original Christian Year Series made for the tree in the Church, members of Ascension always use the butterfly for Easter.

With all this in mind, no home-size or simplified directions for the phoenix are given. Instead, either the butterfly, lily, or some other resurrection symbol is recommended. Directions for the butterfly begin on page 47. The instructions for the lily are the same as for the gladiolus and rose which begin on page 46.

ORIGINAL & PRESENT PHOENIX

Materials: Seed, 2 mm, 3 mm, 5 mm, 6 mm, 3 x 5 mm, 6 x 10 mm, 7 x 11 mm, & 8 x 12 mm pearls; ½" white styrofoam; white & gold screening; white iris glitter; 5 mm gold sequins-by-the-yard; gold vinyl festooning; gold sequin material; white glue; gold & white thread; transparent sticky tape; pipe cleaners; #20 silver color wire; #18 green florist wire; #30 wire.

Directions:

No matter how carefully one may try to follow these directions for the original phoenix, there is only a slight possibility that the original Chrismon can be duplicated. The writer is so certain that it cannot be done that she would not even try. It would be easier to redesign the Chrismon than to try to find the original supplies. These complete directions for the original phoenix are given only so that one can understand the general principles of the bead mosaic method. If these instructions are used, the details must be worked out to suit the beads that can be found.

The search for beads may be greatly eased by making use of a suggestion sent by Chrismon makers of Christ Lutheran Church of San Antonio, Texas. If pearls in some sizes and shapes cannot be found, use white beads sprayed with the pearlized finish that is available from florists.

While the phoenix of legend never existed, it was supposed to resemble an eagle. If the bird that is made looks like an eagle, it will be recognizable as the Resurrection symbol.

* * *

In the bead mosaic method, the beads are set into a bed of shaped styrofoam. Screening is placed behind the styrofoam bed to provide an anchor for attaching the beads. Sometimes wire or thread holds a bead in place. When a wire or thread is pulled tightly against styrofoam, the wire or thread will cut through the foam. The screening behind the foam provides a base which holds thread or wire to prevent its cutting.

When the screen backs white styrofoam, spray the screening with white paint. Then cut out a piece of screening one-fourth inch larger all the way around the drawing of Detail 1 of Figure 48 on page 42. Fold the extra one-fourth inch under to make the screening slightly smaller than Detail 1. The fold keeps the screen from unraveling when something is attached to the edge. After the styrofoam section is cut, attach the screen to its back with one inch U-shaped pipe cleaner pieces.

Cut one-half inch styrofoam by the outline of Detail 1. Carve it to the shape of the bird's head and body in half relief. Feather the edges to a thickness of about one-eighth inch. This is the bed in which the pearls are set.

The body of the phoenix is covered with 7 x 11 mm squared oval pearls. A curved depression, which runs the length of the pearl, gives the effect of a feather. Selection of the beads to use and the manner of manipulating them is a matter of exercising one's imagination and artistic ability.

First place the pearls on a drawing of the body to find the best arrangement to cover the area; the best arrangement is the one that most gives the effect of the thing to be portrayed. Because the styrofoam is curved to make the rounded body, the beads will roll off before the slow drying styrofoam glue will hold them in place. Therefore, when the arrangement is transferred to the body, push each bead slightly into the styrofoam to provide a setting which will hold the pearl until the glue dries. Set all the beads into the body before any are glued in place so that adjustments in placement can be made if necessary. After the large beads are glued in place, glue 2 mm and 3 mm pearls into the larger spaces between the 7 x 11 mm pearls to hide the bare foam. (This method was used to construct the original body of the phoenix, the lamb's head and body, and the dove.)

The beak is a 6 x 10 mm oval pearl; the mouth is a line of gold paint on the pearl as shown on the pattern. Push the beak slightly into the styrofoam. Hold it in place with a straight pin into the head while the seed pearls are stitched on to the head. After the seed pearls are attached, glue the pinned beak in position with styrofoam glue.

The head is made of seed pearls strung on thread. Sew the length of threaded beads to the top of the styrofoam with another thread and needle. Push the beads slightly into the foam as they are attached. If desired, a line of white glue may be put on the foam just before a line of beads is stitched to the foam.

Begin by tying the attaching thread to the screen at the back. Run the thread up through the foam and over the line of beads. Run the thread back through the foam and around a line of the screen; pull it tight before the next stitch. The pattern of the head does not show the pearls. Rather it depicts the threads on which the pearls are strung. They seem closer together on the head around the eye than on the neck because the shaping of the head curves outward. The eye is a 5 mm gold metal bead which is pinned and glued into place.

Constructing the head by sewing strings of beads over a styrofoam base is similar to the way in which the central cross of the Jerusalem Cross in the Basic Series is made. The procedure is used on the following original Chrismons of this Series: the hand, the Epiphany Star, the body and head of the pelican, and the head of the phoenix. (On the chariot sides, the strung beads are sewn directly to the screening.) In all these cases, many small beads of the same size are used to cover a relatively large area. When larger or different size beads are used to cover styrofoam, work them like the body of the phoenix.

After the Chrismon is finished, the wire screening and styrofoam backing should not be seen from the front or side of the symbol. Foam deep enough to provide a bed for large beads may show at the edges between the beads. To cover such spaces, small pearls are glued in as fillers. However, to cover these spaces when small strung beads are used, the last row of beads must be next to, rather than on top of the screening. This is the reason for making the screening base for these designs one-sixteenth to one-eighth inch smaller than the finished outline. Attach the last row of pearls at the edge of the screen to complete the head.

The three lines atop the head are curved pins or wires strung with seed pearls. They form the bird's crest and are glued in place on the same plane as the beak—that is, at the level of the screening. The three lines at the back of the head are made like the crest and attached on the same level. But the crest lines of pearls are separated from each other so that they look like three separate plumes; the pearls at the back of the head lie close together and appear to be a solid triangle.

The tail is composed of seven rows of 6 x 10 mm oval pearls; each row is tipped with a seed pearl. Place a seed pearl in the middle of a length of #30 wire. Fold the wire so that both ends are together. Then run both wire ends through the number of oval beads on that piece of the tail. To attach the row of pearls to the bird, run the two wire ends through the bottom edge of the screen. Twist the wires together to hold behind the body.

* * *

Both wings are woven on wires and attached by wires to the back of the body. The left wing on the pattern shows the pearls which make up the weave; the right wing pictures the attachment and weaving wires. The small end beads and small crossovers in the D section are 2 mm pearls; the larger rounds are 6 mm pearls; the ovals are 6 x 10 mm and 8 x 12 mm pearls.

Bend a length of #18 stiff green florist wire to the shape shown by the A wire. Begin at B by making a small circle; shape the wire up to the border beads; bend it to lie behind the beaded circle at A. Then shape the wire down along the other side of circle B and across the back of the bird. On the other side of the body, make the AB frame in reverse.

The C lines of pearls are like the tail section except that a shaped piece of #20 wire runs through the pearls along with the #30 wires. Shape two pieces of #20 wire as shown on the right side of the pattern. Note that piece F fits into two lines of beads; the other pieces, G, in only one line. String each C wing line as directed for the tail pieces and as shown on the C pattern. Pull the wires tight. Then insert the shaped F and G wires to their full length. Attach the #30 wire to the florist wire at the top by twisting the leftover #30 wire around the adjoining heavier wires to hold.

Bend a piece of #20 silver colored wire to the shape of the line of 6 mm pearls marked E. To keep beads from falling off, make a sharp turn one-eighth inch from the wire end. Place a 6 mm pearl in the middle of a length of #30 wire; run the wired pearl over the shaped #20 wire. Run a second 6 mm pearl over the #20 wire and both ends of the #30 wire. String an 8 x 12 mm and a 2 mm pearl on one end of the #30 wire; run the #30 wire back through the 8 x 12 mm pearl to the #30 wire. Then run a 6 mm pearl over the #20 wire and the two #30 wires. Pull the wires tight. String an 8 x 12 mm and a 2 mm pearl on one #30 wire. Continue to string the beads in like manner until seven 6 mm beads are strung.

Bend the #20 wire at a right angle as shown, String a 5 mm pearl over all the wires. Make another right angle bend in the #20 wire. Shape it to the A wire behind the body. At the middle of the A wire behind the body, bend the #20 wire at a right angle so that it lies flat behind the body. Cut the wire off to a 2 inch length. Make another E section, a reverse of the first. Join the E and A wires by twisting the leftover #30 wire around the E and A wires at their points of contact. Then twist the #30 wires around the two E wires where they touch behind the body.

Weave the D section on #30 wire. The right pattern side diagrams the weave which begins at

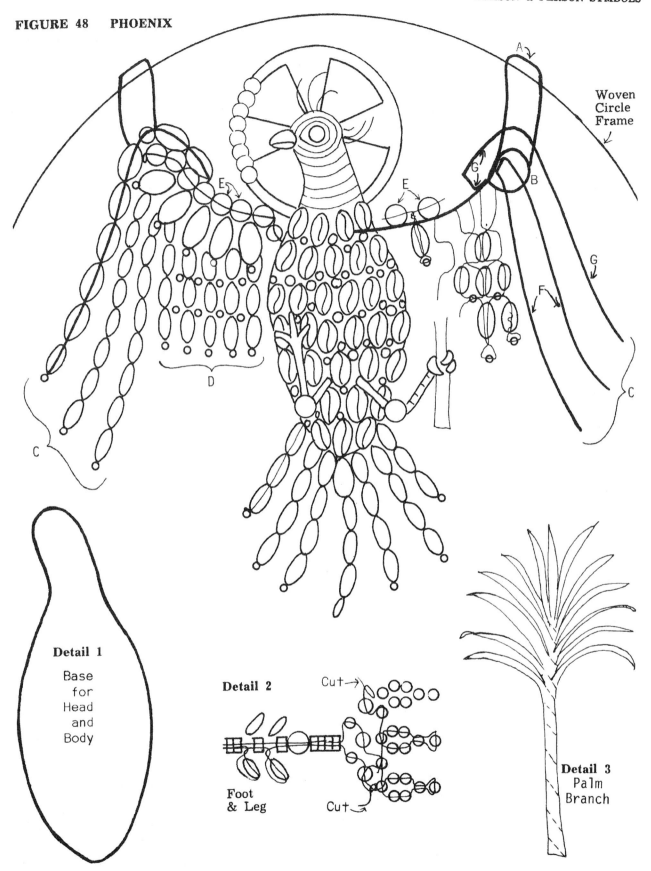

FIGURE 48 PHOENIX

the bottom beads. Notice that the crossovers are 2 mm pearls and that the lengthwise beads are 6 x 10 mm pearls. Twist each of the two outer bottom 2 mm pearls to hold at the end of a piece of #30 wire. Twist each of the three 2 mm bottom center beads at the middle of a length of #30 wire which is twice as long as the end pieces. Weave the pearls by rows up to the A wire. Weave another D section which is opposite to the first. Attach the D weaves to the wings by twisting the excess #30 wire around wire A and circle B. Finally, wire the pair of wings to the screen behind the body. Use #30 wire to fasten the A and E wire ends in place.

* * *

Detail 2 shows the beads and wiring diagram of a leg and foot. The smallest beads are seed pearls; the larger ones, 3 mm pearls. The knee is a 5 mm pearl; the leg beads, white satin bugles; the upper leg feathers, 3 x 6 mm pearls. Weave the foot by starting with a length of #30 wire at each toe. Attach the legs to the body by pushing the leftover #30 wire through the body and twisting it around the back screening.

Make the triradiant nimbus of 5 mm gold sequins-by-the-yard sewn to gold screening. Fasten it to the back of the head with U-shaped #30 wire pieces dipped in white glue.

The palm branch is gold vinyl festooning spiraled around a length of pipe cleaner. Detail 3 shows the full-size palm. Tape the ends of the festooning to the pipe cleaner with transparent sticky tape. Place the palm in the foot and wrap the talons around it to hold.

Cover the screen and wires behind the phoenix with white iris glitter. Hang the bird in its circle by wiring the bends in the A wire to the frame wires with #30 wire. Twist a piece of #30 wire on the center tail where it joins the body. Fasten one end to the circle on one side, the other end at the frame on the opposite side.

FIGURE 49

Cut the flames from gold foil or sequin material by the pattern on Figure 49 above. To reinforce the bottom, apply a layer of transparent sticky tape along the back of the bottom edge. With a stylus, score the gold material along the dashed pattern lines to break up the solid gold look to a flickering flame effect. Use a compass point to punch the holes in the base of the flames at the tiny circles.

Place the bottom of the flames under the circle frame and below the bird's tail. Spiral gold thread around the circle and through the holes in the flames to hold the latter firmly against the woven circle.

PELICAN-IN-HER-PIETY

Photographs: Original & Present, page 65; Simplified & Half-Size, page 58.

SIMPLIFIED & HALF-SIZE PELICAN

Materials: ½" & 1" white styrofoam; rigid white fiberglass material; white iris glitter; gold sequin material; gold seed & 6 mm or 3 mm beads; about 3 x 6 mm red stones; gold stretch mesh; white glue; styrofoam hangers; #30 wire.

Directions:

Carve the pelican from one inch styrofoam by the pattern on Figure 50 on page 44. (Use one-half inch foam and the pattern on Figure 51 on page 45 for the half-size bird.) Note that the underside of the pelican is depicted.

Cut the beak from gold sequin material by the Detail 1 pattern. Crease and fold it along its vertical dotted lines to make three sides of the beak. Push the top of the beak into the head of the pelican so that the bottom touches the breast as shown on the pattern. The beak cuts into the foam to line D. Remove the beak. Make the eye depression with a 6 mm gold bead. (Use a 3 mm bead for the home-size.) Cover the entire pelican with white iris glitter. Glue the beak and eye in place.

If red stones about 3 x 6 mm in size cannot be found for the blood, paint pearls with red fingernail polish. Glue the drops of blood high enough on the breast to show over the heads of the little birds.

A cruciform rather than the usual triradiant nimbus is recommended for the pelican. Cut the nimbus from gold sequin material. Pin and glue it to the back of the head. Insert a styrofoam hanger at the top back of each wing.

Carve the basket from a one by two by 4½ inch piece of styrofoam as shown on Details 2 and 2A. (Use a one by two by one-half inch piece for the half-size.) Hollow it out so that it is about one-half inch thick. Then, between the thumb and fingers, press the sides and bottom to a thickness of about one-fourth inch. Cover the basket, inside and out, with gold stretch mesh. Sew the mesh in place where necessary.

Cut the bodies and wings of the small birds out of white fiberglass by the patterns. Glue the wings to the bodies at the X's. Glue the gold seed bead eyes in place. Run three lengths of

FIGURE 50
PELICAN-IN-HER-PIETY

SEASON & PERSON SYMBOLS

FIGURE 51

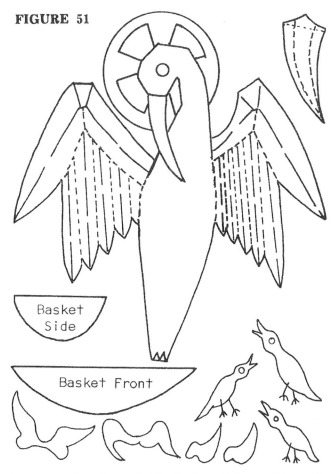

Carve the head and body of the pelican from one inch styrofoam. While the full-size pattern may be used as a guide, the angles should be rounded off. In addition, curve the head outward so that it is in the full round. The back is flat from the middle of the neck to the base. The carving must be slightly smaller than the desired finished symbol.

Cut white screening one-fourth inch larger than the back of the bird and the thick upper part of the wings. Fold the edges of the screen to make it one-eighth inch smaller than the foam. Attach the screening to the back with U-shaped pipe cleaner pieces. Carve and attach one-half inch foam for the upper wing bases.

Weave the bird's beak of gold glass bugles. Start the weave of the round beak at its point in a manner similar to the parallel bugle weave. At the junction of the beak to the head, cut the beak wires to one inch lengths. Push them into the styrofoam base of the head. Glue them in place after the head is beaded.

Cover the entire head and neck and the sides and front of the body with white satin bugles strung on thread. Sew and glue the beads in place where necessary. Glue in red stones for the blood and a 6 mm gold bead for the front eye.

Weave the lower wings by the parallel bugle weave method. Begin at the tips, which are seed pearls. When the woven part of each section of the wing is complete, run the wire ends through the lower edge of the screening back of the upper wing. Twist the wires to hold the section in place. After all the lower wing pieces are attached to the screen, attach the carved upper wing sections to the screening with pipe cleaner pieces. Then cover the styrofoam with strung white satin bugles. Cover the wires and screening on the back with white iris glitter.

* * *

Carve the small birds from one inch white styrofoam. Make their legs and eyes as directed for the simplified birds.

For the nest, string gold seed beads on #30 wire lengths. Use a straight line anchor to hold the first and last beads on the wire. Then weave a basket of these beaded wires. Consult a beginner's book on weaving to find a pattern. Any type weave may be used.

Set and glue the base of the pelican into the back of the basket. Run a U-shaped four inch pipe cleaner piece over a beaded wire of the basket up into the base of the pelican. Fasten the leg wires of the little birds around wires of the nest so that the birds stand at the front.

Make a cruciform nimbus of gold wire screen and 5 mm gold sequins-by-the-yard. Pin and glue the center of the nimbus at the back eye of the pelican.

Hang the completed symbol in its border by four #30 wires. Fasten one at each side back of the nest; attach one to the screening of each upper wing.

beading wire through the body. String gold seed beads on them to make the legs and feet as shown on Detail 3. Bend the leg wires so that the bird appears to stand. (Or carve the birds' bodies from styrofoam and glue the fiberglass wings and beaded feet in place.)

Arrange the birds on the edge of the basket so that their actions can be seen. Run the leftover wires from the feet through glue into the styrofoam. Glue the large pelican to the bottom of the basket with white glue. Then run a two inch length of glue-covered pipe cleaner up through the basket. Suspend the birds and the basket in its beaded frame by the two hangers in the wings and the two basket hangers.

ORIGINAL & PRESENT PELICAN

Materials: White satin & gold bugles; pearl & gold seed beads; 6 mm gold bead; 3 x 6 mm red beads; 1" & ½" white styrofoam; 5 mm gold sequins-by-the-yard; white & gold wire screening; white pipe cleaners; #30 hair wire.

Directions:

The head, body, and upper wings of the original pelican are made by the strung bead mosaic method; the lower wings are woven by the parallel bugle weave of the flames. See page 52 for directions in this procedure.

45

GLADIOLUS, ROSE, LILY

Photographs: Gladiolus, page 30; Rose, Page 32.

In the interpretation of the Christian Year Series, the meaning of each of these symbols is given to help in the decision of which to choose. It is possible, however, and even probable that practical considerations will determine the selection. So be it! It will not be the first time that one has been forced to look at a truth because it was the only thing that worked in a specific situation.

When the full-size Chrismons are wanted, the gladiolus is the easiest Christmas symbol to use; if the half-size Christian Year Series is constructed, the rose works best because in its natural size it is closest to the dimensions of the other symbols. The lily may be chosen for Easter for similar practical reasons.

* * *

The following instructions are the same for any of the original, present, and simplified flowers in either half or full-size. But one need not be limited to making blossoms in the Christian Year Series by the suggested method.

These symbols can be made with dipping film for which directions are given under the God Man wreath on page 46 in *Chrismons for Every Day*. Beaded flowers which have been recently promoted in craft groups are suitable too. Possibilities also include other fabric, paper, and other fiber flowers. One who has skill in one or more of these procedures should feel free to adapt any of them to these symbols. On the other hand, the specific instructions that follow probably present the easiest method.

Materials: White polyethylene flower; assorted gold and/or pearl rocaille, bugle, and/or 3 mm to 5 mm beads; gold sequin material, gold-backed paper, or gold colored metallic leaf and adhesive and/or gold paint; #30 hair wire.

Directions:

To make either the rose, gladiolus, or lily, begin with a white polyethylene flower from a 5 & 10 cent store or florist. (Some people think that a Chrismon tree is made to show only what can be done with one's own hands. Not at all! There is no objection to using anything that today's merchants can supply to help to tell the story that Chrismons proclaim.)

Examination of a polyethylene flower shows that it can be taken apart and rearranged to make a flower or group of florets in the wanted proportions. The modification, of course, must retain the essential characteristics of the blossom. If the gladiolus is chosen, let the drawing of Figure 52 on page 47, which is pictured about half-size, be the guide. Figure 53 on the same page is the approximate pattern for a rose to fit the half-size Series.

Take the polyethylene flower apart. Rearrange the leaves and petals on the stem to make a symbol of the needed size. Discard the excess parts. Separate the flower parts again. Use the white parts of the blossoms as they are. Or the white petals may be sprayed with a pearlized finish to enrich them.

* * *

From pearl and/or gold bugle, rocaille, and seed to 5 mm size beads, make substitutes for the colored centers of the blossoms. If help is needed in this procedure, see "Flowers" on page 18 in *Chrismons for Every Day*. Substitutes for the green cups may be made from 20 mm or larger gold findings. The stems can be made of 5 mm or larger gold beads. However, both the stems and cup may also be made in gold by any of the following methods which are used for the leaves.

The three procedures that follow explain how to change green leaves, stems, and cups to gold. Use whichever one seems best.

1) Spray the green parts with gold paint. While this is the easiest method, the resulting gold is dull. Furthermore, it is not durable; paint adheres poorly to polyethylene. One must be careful that the paint is not rubbed off when the flower is reassembled.

2) Spray the parts gold. After the flower is reassembled, gold leaf the exposed parts. This is the method for the original gladiolus which is pictured on page 30. While the gold still is not too durable, it is not handled as much after the final finish is applied. In addition, the gold leaf is rich in appearance. Now one can have this finish without the expense of gold. A metallic leaf is available which has the same appearance as real gold.

3) Make substitute leaves from gold sequin material or gold-backed paper. These leaves are reasonably durable and have the finish to match the other Chrismons. Use the artificial leaves from the flower as the pattern. Score the veins on the leaf with a stylus or a ball point pen.

If sequin material is used, extend the leaf stem to a circle which slips over the main stem; reinforce the circle with transparent sticky tape. If gold-backed paper is used, glue a flower-making wire between the two layers of paper (gold side out) for the midvein and stem. Make the cups in three or four pieces and glue them around the base of the flower. The rose that is shown on page 32 has sequin material leaves.

After making gold leaves and parts by whichever method or combination of methods is desired, reassemble the flower and leaves with the new parts. Spiral one-half to one-fourth inch strips of gold-backed paper around the flower stem and glue them in place. Attach three or four #30 wires as needed to the stem and/or the petals and/or the leaves to hold the flower properly in the beaded circle.

SEASON & PERSON SYMBOLS

FIGURE 52 GLADIOLUS (Half actual size)   FIGURE 53   ROSE

BUTTERFLY

Photograph: Half-Size, page 38.

Separate drawings of the butterfly's parts are given only for the half-size pattern. Adapt these directions to the full-size design.

If desired, this symbol can be made with dipping film. Directions for that procedure are on page 48 in *Chrismons for Every Day*.

HALF-SIZE BUTTERFLY

Materials: Stiff white fiberglass, transparent plastic, or other clear or white material (the pictured butterfly is gathered lace); pearl and/or gold beads from seed to 8 mm (full-size, to 12 mm); white iris and/or gold glitter; white or clear glue; beading wire.

Directions:

Cut out the butterfly wings, Detail 2 on Figure 54 on page 48, from white fiberglass. (If the wings are cut from transparent plastic, see the angel wing directions in the *Advanced Series* for specific directions on handling the material.)

Put lines of white iris glitter on the dashed lines and edges of the wings. Cut the Alpha and Omega and/or other wanted decorations from gold foil, sequin material, or paper; glue a row of 5 mm gold sequins along the wing edges as shown.

This simple design can be varied in numerous ways or original ideas may be developed. Any butterfly pattern of the right size may be used. Gold glitter can substitute for the white; or both colors may be combined. Use various shapes of gold and/or white iris sequins or sequin material cutouts. If embroidery is a talent, gold and/or white threads may elaborate the design.

For an antenna, center a seed bead on a 15 inch piece of beading wire. Fold the wire; string gold or pearl seed, bugle, or rocaille beads over both wire ends for the antenna length. Make another antenna.

Run the wires from both antennae through the head bead and then the body beads in order from the head to the tail. Run only one wire from each antenna through the end seed tail bead. Run these same two wires back through all the body beads in reverse order; tighten the wires. As shown on the patterns, various bead combinations may make up the head and body.

Place the center of the wings under the body. Lay the wires from the tail under the wings to hold the latter next to the body; twist the wires around the wires between the head and body beads. Again lay the wires under the wings; twist the wires to hold around the wires between the tail and body. Hang the butterfly in its circle by the two wires at the head and the two wires at the tail.

The butterfly may be varied by folding the wings back to simulate a butterfly at rest as shown on Detail 4. Fold the wings back before adding them to the body. Run the hanger wires from the body up between the wings.

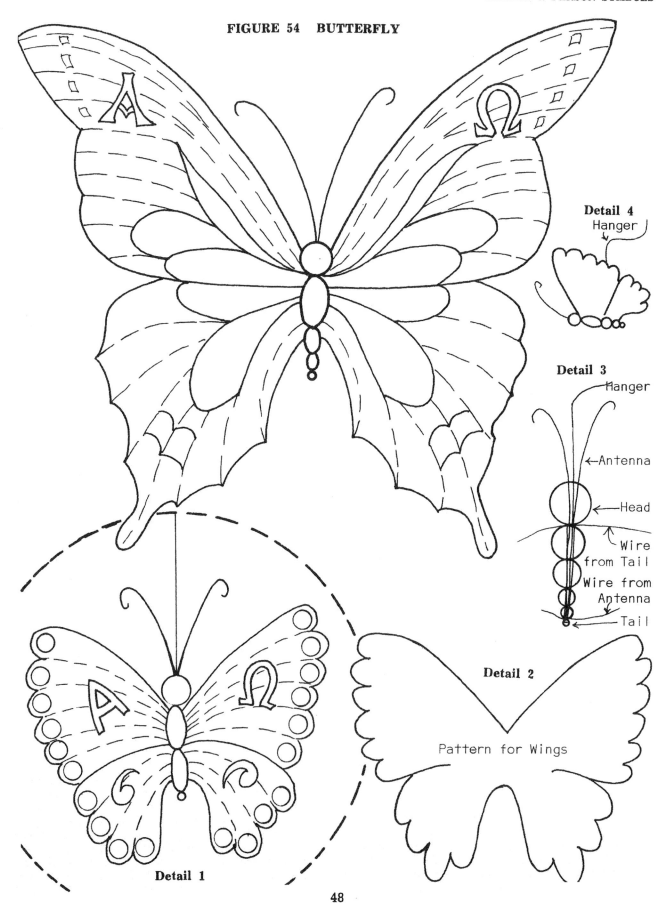

SEASON & PERSON SYMBOLS

SCROLL WITH PROPHECY

Photographs: Original & Full-Size, page 38; Half-size, page 50.

ORIGINAL, FULL-SIZE SCROLL

Materials: Gold foil or gold-backed paper; 1½" white styrofoam; 5 x 7 mm to 6 x 10 mm pearls; 3 mm & seed pearls; pipe cleaners; gold beading wire; #30 wire; sequin pins; white glue.

Directions:

Cut a piece of gold foil 4½ by 12 inches in size. Place the letter pattern on Detail 1 of Figure 55 on page 50 on top of the foil. The gold side of the foil should be up; the tops of the letters should be 2¾ inches from the top of the foil. With the gold side still up, fold the foil under one-fourth inch from the top edge and 2½ inches from the bottom edge.

Cut two 5½ inch pieces of pipe cleaner. Glue a pearl, ranging in size from 4 x 7 mm to 6 x 10 mm, on each end of both pieces so that 4½ inches in the middle of each pipe cleaner is free. Place one length of pipe cleaner in the fold at the top of the foil as shown on Detail 2. Press the foil flat and sew thread through the foil and around the pipe cleaner to hold the cleaner firmly in the fold. Attach the other cleaner in the bottom fold in the same manner. (If gold-backed paper is used instead of the foil, glue two pieces of paper, 4½ by 9¾ inches, together. Fold them over one-fourth inch from each end. Glue a pearl-tipped pipe cleaner into each fold.)

Carve and shape a piece of ½ by 4 by 5½ inch styrofoam as shown on Detail 3. Position it behind the foil as shown on Detail 4 and the arrows between Details 1 and 2.

* * *

String seed pearls on beading wire to make the individual letters of "be called." Use 3 mm pearls to form the remainder of the quotation. To string the letters, start with one bead on a piece of #30 wire. Run both ends of the wire through the next pearl. Continue stringing the required number of beads and shape them to make the desired letter. Some letters will require looping a second wire over the wire between previously strung beads. Leave one-half inch end pieces of wire on each letter. These wire ends run, like pins, through the foil into the styrofoam backing to help hold the letters in place. Detail 5 shows the placement of pearls and wires on a representative group of letters. Use them as a guide to work out the number of pearls and wires that are needed for the other letters. The circles on the pattern are single pearls. Each is held in place with a sequin pin.

Place each pearl letter over its corresponding letter on the foil. Punch holes through the foil with a needle to allow the wires to pierce the foil at the proper points.

Smear styrofoam glue over the curved surface of the styrofoam. Place the gold foil on it. Pin the pearl dots in place with sequin pins. Then letter by letter, place a bit of household cement on the letter impression in the foil. Position the corresponding pearl letter on top; run the letter's wires through the foil into the styrofoam. Finally, push the letter firmly against the foil.

Roll the excess foil of the scroll beyond the styrofoam backing forward around the bottom pipe cleaner and back around the top pipe cleaner. See Detail 4. Roll the foil tightly enough so that it holds its curved position.

Insert a styrofoam hanger in each of the four corners of the styrofoam back. Suspend the scroll in its beaded circle frame at a slight angle by the four wires from the four styrofoam hangers.

SIMPLIFIED SCROLL

The only difference between the simplified and the original scroll is in the construction of the letters. For the simplified design, the letters are drawn in glue (white or Duco type) and sprinkled with white iris glitter.

After the styrofoam backing is shaped, smear white glue over its curved surface. With a needle and white thread, sew the foil to the styrofoam backing so that the foil is flat against the foam. One stitch of the thread should follow a line, on top of the foil, of each of the traced letters. Since glue does not stick well to foil, the thread is necessary to anchor the foil to the styrofoam and to hold the glue and glitter letters in place.

Run a thin line of glue on a letter; be certain that the letter's threads are covered. Sprinkle the wet glue with white iris glitter. Let it dry.

While the sprinkled letters are not as even as the pearl letters, they are quite legible. Be careful in applying the glue. Pick or cut off any excess glitter after the glue is dry.

HALF-SIZE SCROLL

Make the half-size scroll like either the simplified or original ornament by the patterns on Detail 6 of Figure 55. The following size alterations should also be made: The foil is 2½ by 6½ inches in size; the tops of the letters are traced onto the foil 1½ inches from the top. Seed pearls are used to make all the letters. Note the side view of the ½ by 2⅜ by 2⅛ inch styrofoam back. The pipe cleaner pieces should be 3⅛ inches long.

FIGURE 55 SCROLL with PROPHECY

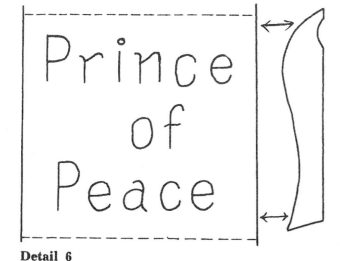

SEASON & PERSON SYMBOLS

FIGURE 56   SEVEN-TONGUED FLAME

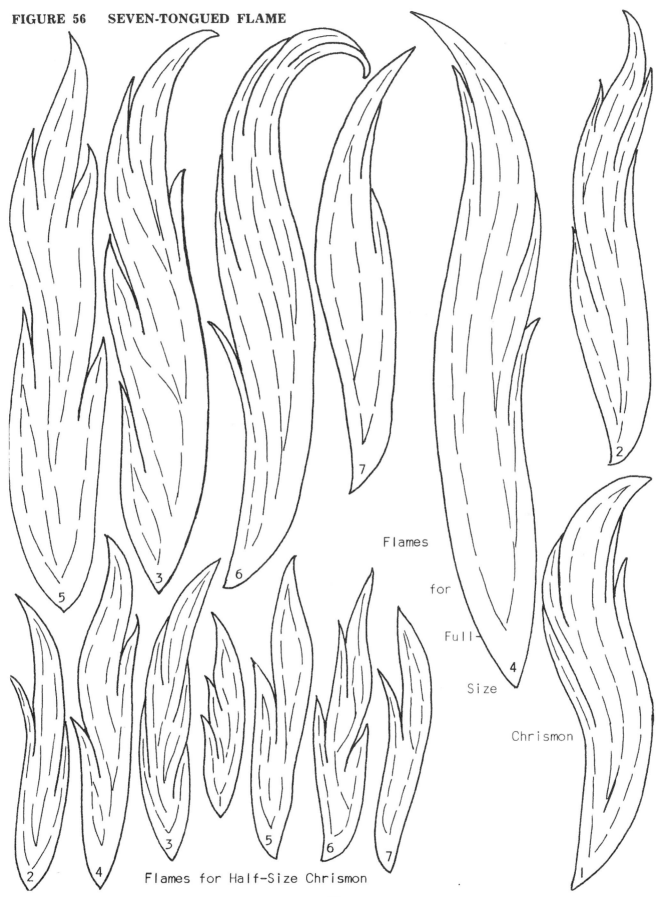

SEASON & PERSON SYMBOLS

SEVEN-TONGUED FLAME

Photographs: Original & Present, page 26; Half-Size & Simplified, page 38.

SIMPLIFIED & HALF-SIZE FLAMES

Materials: Gold sequin material; 5 mm gold sequins; gold beading wire; gold glass rocailles; Duco type cement; beading wire.

Directions:

Cut the seven flames from gold sequin material or two pieces of gold-backed paper glued together with the gold side out. Use the seven large flames on Figure 56 on page 51 for the full-size Chrismon, the smaller ones for the home-size symbol. Notice that the solid cutting line around some of the flames on the pattern extends far into the flame.

Roll, twist, and turn the flames and/or their parts to give them depth and a live, dancing effect. Scoring with a stylus along the dashed lines (sometimes on one side, sometimes on the other) helps break up the flat look. Pulling an end of a flame between the thumb and the back of a scissors blade also helps. Work each flame individually to get as much twist as possible.

Each flame is numbered at its base to show how it is joined. Flame #1 goes on the left; #7 to the right; the others follow consecutively in between. Place and arrange them so that the overlapping ends form a V. Glue the ends of the flames together so that the free ends fan out as shown on Figure 57 below.

Center a gold rocaille on a 15 inch length of gold beading wire. Run both ends of the wire through a 5 mm gold sequin and then through a hole punched in the top of flame #4 as shown at A. Run both wires through another sequin and rocaille. Straight line anchor the rocaille as close to the flame as possible. The wire ends become the B hangers. In like manner, run another piece of beading wire through a rocaille, a sequin, and the glued-together bottom V section of the flames. The wire ends become the hanging wires.

Glue 5 mm gold sequins to the front and back of the area where the flames are glued together.

ORIGINAL & PRESENT SEVEN-TONGUED FLAME

Materials: Gold glass bugle and rocaille beads; 5 mm gold sequins; gold beading wire.

Directions:

The original flames are woven of gold bugles of varied lengths on gold beading wire. The patterns are the same as those for the simplified foil flames. Cuts into the flames are woven into them. The finished flames are bent, shaped, and twisted to give the dancing, flickering effect of live fire.

The basic principle of the flame weave is shown on Figure 58 at the right. The greatly enlarged diagram shows the beads loosely strung. The actual weave must be tight. Begin at the bottom on beading wire. Add wires as diagramed to widen the flame. A flame is held together by running a wire from a bead in one line through a bead in an adjoining line about every four bugles. Flame ends can be separated or cut by not carrying wires from one line of beads into the adjoining line. If more information on this weave is wanted, see the construction of the original Spirit circle under the "Parable Balls" in *Chrismons: Advanced Series*.

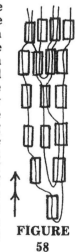

FIGURE 58

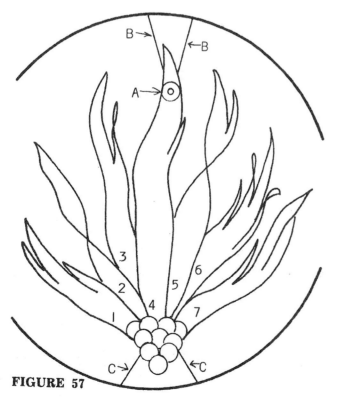

FIGURE 57

After each flame is woven, twist and shape it so that its plane breaks into flickering surfaces. Place and wire the bases of the seven flames together so that their ends converge in a V. Attach the same type of hanging wires as described for the simplified flames but omit the sequins. Hang the flames in their border. Five mm gold sequins may be glued to cover any wires at the base.

Light shines through these beads. Therefore, if wanted, some lights may be concentrated behind the triangular base of the symbol when it is hung on the tree. When the lights are burning, a glow will seem to emit from the flames.

SEASON & PERSON SYMBOLS

FIGURE 59 FIERY CHARIOT

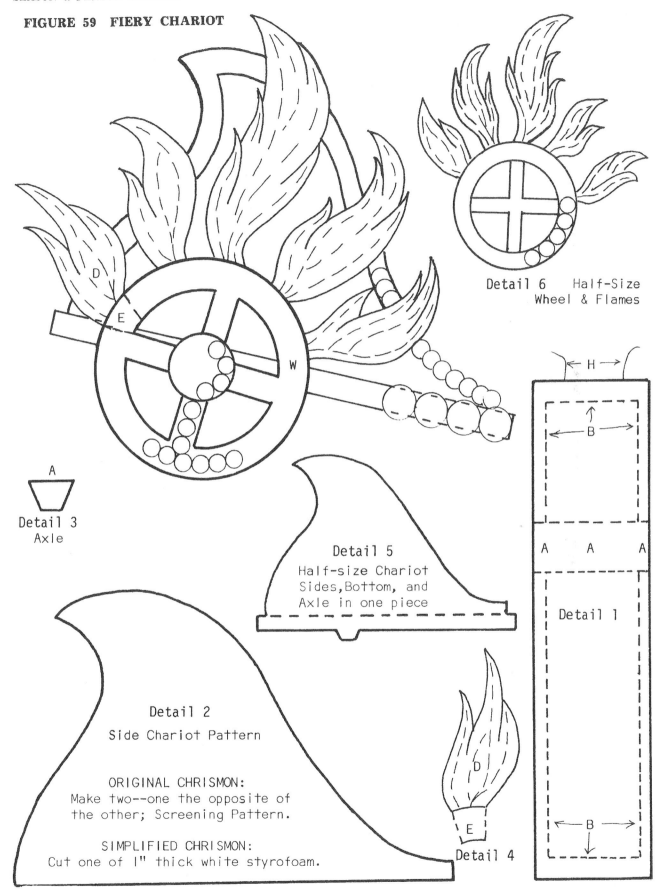

FIERY CHARIOT

Photographs: Original & Present, left on page 55; Half-Size Simplified, right on page 55.

SIMPLIFIED FULL-SIZE CHARIOT

Materials: ½″ & 1″ white styrofoam; gold-backed paper; gold sequin material; 5 mm half-round pearls; 5 mm gold sequins-by-the-yard; 8 mm gold sequins; gold bugle beads; sequin pins; gold paint; styrofoam glue; #30 hair wire.

Directions:

The outside solid line of Detail 1 of Figure 59 on page 53 is the chariot floor pattern; cut it from one-fourth inch thick styrofoam. Detail 2 is the chariot body pattern; cut it from one inch foam. Cut out the axle from one-half inch foam by the side view pattern of Detail 3 and the top view at A on Detail 1. Glue the axle, base, and chariot body together.

Cover the chariot completely with styrofoam glue to fill the pores; when the glue is dry, smooth it out with a knife blade and slight pressure. Paint the chariot with glue again; once more smooth the surface. Again cover the symbol with glue. Then spray paint the entire chariot gold. The Fish in a Circle in the Basic Series gives complete directions for this procedure.

Glue two styrofoam hangers in the back of the chariot body; place one at the top and another at the bottom back. Glue two more hangers into the front edge of the base at points H.

Glue and pin a row of 5 mm gold sequins-by-the-yard on the side and top edges of the chariot sides as shown on the main pattern. Glue 8 mm sequins all around the edge of the base.

Glue two pieces of gold-backed paper (the gold sides out) together. From this paper, cut out four wheels by the complete pattern. From gold sequin material, cut out two each of the five flames that extend from the wheel. Note flame D on the large pattern and Detail 4 to see how a tab, E, is added to each flame to provide an attachment point. With a stylus, score each flame along the dashed lines to break up the flat look of the surface.

Glue one set of flames between two wheels so that the flames emerge as shown. Glue the other flames between the other two wheels. Glue 5 mm half-round pearls in the middle of the outer circle of the wheel, on each spoke, and around the outer edge of the inner circle. Put a drop of white glue on the axle; then run a straight pin through an 8 mm pearl, through the center of the wheel, and into the axle. Glue the other wheel on the opposite axle end in like manner.

Suspend the chariot in its circle border by its four hangers so that it appears to be traveling upward. Before the hangers are permanently attached, string gold bugle beads over each front hanger to the point where it joins the beaded circle.

SIMPLIFIED HALF-SIZE CHARIOT, I

The first method of constructing the simplified half-size chariot is like the full-size directions except for the following changes:

1) Notice that the half-size pattern allows the body, base, and axle to be cut in one piece.

2) Each wheel is cut in one piece with its flames. Either gold sequin material or gold-backed paper may be used.

3) Use only 5 mm sequins around the chariot's edges; use a 6 mm pearl to attach the wheel.

SIMPLIFIED HALF-SIZE CHARIOT, II

While this pictured Chrismon is half-size, the following directions may be adapted to the full-size symbol.

Materials: Embossed gold-backed paper; 2 different designs ¼″ to ½″ metallic gold braid or foil edging or trim; ¼″ metallic cord; 5 mm half round pearls; 6 mm pearls; gold 16 mm sunburst and 8 mm cup sequins; gold sequin material; cardboard about 1/16″ thick; gold sequin pins; #30 hair wire.

Directions:

The two sides and floor of the chariot are cut in one piece. Make the pattern by cutting out two side pieces. Lay them down with their bases toward each other, parallel, and exactly 1 1/16 inches apart. The fronts of both cutouts must face in the same direction. The two sides with the space between them is the pattern. Cut it out of cardboard about 1/16 inch thick. Score one side of the cardboard along the lines at the base of each side.

Plain metallic gold-backed paper may be used. But such paper embossed with a design is generally more attractive. Glue the paper to cover the chariot sides and bottom of the unscored side of the cardboard. With the scored side out, bend each side of the chariot up along the scored line. Then glue gold-backed paper on the outside of the two sides.

Cut two more pieces of cardboard to fit under the floor of the chariot. Glue them together. Cover one side with gold-backed paper. Glue the uncovered side to the bottom of the chariot.

Glue one of the metallic gold braids along the side and top edges of the chariot sides. Glue and pin the other gold braid all around the base. Pins can be inserted into the middle of the pieces of cardboard.

Make the wheels like the simplified half-size wheels. Cut a piece of one-fourth inch gold cord to fit across the bottom of the chariot as the axle. Run a straight pin through a 6 mm pearl, an 8 mm cup sequin, a 16 mm sunburst sequin, the center of the wheel and flames, glue on the end

SEASON & PERSON SYMBOLS

of the axle, and into the axle. Glue and pin (up into the cardboard side) the axle in place. Attach four hanging wires by twisting an end of #30 wire around one of the braids or through a hole punched through the cardboard with a needle.

ORIGINAL & PRESENT CHARIOT

Materials: Gold screening; ½" white styrofoam; gold sequin material; gold-backed paper; 5 mm gold sequins-by-the-yard; 8 mm gold sequins; gold seed, rocaille, bugle, 4 mm, & 6 mm beads; 8 mm & 4 x 8 mm pearls; gold thread; #30 hair wire; gold sequin pins; styrofoam glue.

Directions:

Cut two pieces of gold screening one-fourth inch larger than Detail 2 on the pattern. Fold the edges of the screening under so that the screen is about one-sixteenth inch smaller than the pattern.

Tie the end of a piece of gold thread to an edge of the screening. String several rocailles on the thread. Lay the beads over the folded-in edge of the screening; loop the thread around a line of the screening to hold the beads in place. String more rocailles on the thread; lay them on the screening; loop the thread around the screening. Continue to "embroider" the chariot side until the screening is completely covered with gold glass rocailles. Bead both chariot sides in this way. Sew and/or glue two rows of 5 mm gold sequins-by-the-yard around the top and sides of the rocaille covered screen.

* * *

Cut the base of the chariot from one-fourth inch thick styrofoam by the solid outer line of the Detail 1 pattern; cut another piece, the floor, from one fourth inch styrofoam by the dashed B pattern line. Cut axle A by the Detail 1 and Detail 3 patterns. Pin and glue gold-backed paper to cover the bottom and sides only of the axle, the bottom and sides only of the base, and the top and ends only of the floor.

Glue the inside bottom edges of each chariot side to the sides of the floor. Center and glue the floor on the base as diagramed on the Detail 1 pattern. Pin and glue the axle under the base. Pin and glue a row of 8 mm gold sequins all around the edge of the base.

The wheels are woven on #30 wire to approximate the size of the simplified wheels. For the outer circle, use 6 mm gold beads circled with gold seed beads. Run two #30 wires through a 6 mm bead; string seeds on each wire to circle back around the 6 mm bead; run the wires through the 6 mm bead again and in the same direction as they first went through the bead. String another 6 mm bead on both wires; string seed beads on each wire; run the wires through the 6 mm bead again. String another 6 mm bead on both wires. Continue to string beads in the same way until the outer rim of the wheel is complete. Weave the spokes of 4 mm and seed beads in like manner. The center of the wheel is woven of 4 x 8 mm pearls and gold seed beads.

After the wheels are completed, run a pin through an 8 mm pearl, the center of the wheel, through white glue, and into the end of the axle.

Make the flames of gold sequin material like those for the simplified design. Glue them in place behind the wheels. Twist hanger wires to hold around the screening at approximately the same places as directed for the simplified chariot. Bead the two front wires with gold glass bugles before the symbol is hung in its circle.

INDIVIDUAL STARS WITH CHALICE, BOOK, OR SHELL

Because recently developed construction methods for the stars are more attractive and easier to use than the original procedures, the latter are no longer explained. Only one improvement is suggested over the simplest way of making these symbols—after the chalice and shell are painted gold, apply gold colored metallic leaf to cover the gold paint.

Outside of the pattern sizes, there is little difference between the construction of the full and half-size stars. Either size may be cut from one or one-half inch styrofoam. (While the original stars are one-half inch thick, the writer prefers the present one inch symbols.) All other construction details are the same for the designs except for the chalice; its construction and decorations may be varied.

Photographs: Original, Full-Size Stars—Chalice on Six-point Star, Shell on Eight-point Star, Book on Seven-point Star—all on page 58.

GENERAL DIRECTIONS FOR THE STARS

Materials: ½" or 1" white styrofoam; crystal, white, or white iris glitter; styrofoam glue; styrofoam hangers.

Directions:

Extend any incomplete star pattern lines to their peaks. Then cut the star from one-half or one inch thick white styrofoam. While the star can be used in its flat state, carving it like the five-point Epiphany Star will improve its appearance. After cutting the star's face to accept its symbol (cup, shell, or book), cover the surfaces of the star with white iris glitter.

Glue a styrofoam hanger into the back of the star at the X. On the six-point star, glue two extra hangers—one just to the upper right, the other to the lower left of the X. Glue extra hangers to the upper left and lower right of the X hanger on the eight-point star. The seven-point star has only one hanger at the X mark.

SHELL ON EIGHT-POINT STAR

Materials: Scallop shell 3½" to 4" high (or about 2" for the half-size); teardrop shaped pearl or crystal beads—about 8 x 16 mm for the full-size, 4 x 8 mm for the half-size; gold paint; clear acrylic spray; white glue; gold metallic leaf & adhesive if desired.

Directions:

Be certain that the shell is clean and dry. (Baking dish shells are ideal.) Paint the shell gold. If desired, apply gold metallic leaf over the paint. Glue three teardrop pearl or crystal beads to the inside lower edge of the shell as shown on Figure 61 on page 57 for the full-size shell or on the background pattern on page 7 for the half-size. Spray the shell and pearls with a clear acrylic plastic finish to prevent tarnish.

Cut out and carve the full-size eight-point styrofoam star by the colored background pattern on page 7 (or the half-size by the background pattern on this page) and the General Star Directions. Place the shell on the star with their X's superimposed. Carve out the star's center so that the shell's convex side sits about three-eighths inch inside the star. Apply glitter to all the star's surfaces. Finally glue the shell into its hole in the star with white glue.

CHALICE ON SIX-POINT STAR

Materials: 2" or 3" white styrofoam; white glue; wafer or flat pearl about 1¼" in diameter or a 20 mm white iris bangle for the half-size; gold paint; gold colored metallic leaf & adhesive if wanted; metallic gold braids & trims as desired; half-round pearls of varied sizes if wanted; clear acrylic spray finish; pipe cleaner pieces.

Directions:

Carve the cup from two or three inch styrofoam by the full-size pattern shown on Figure 62 on page 57 or the half-size pattern on the background of page 24. (Styrofoam pieces can be glued together to make a three inch block.) The best pattern is a real chalice. Cut a slice out of the flat top of the chalice to accept the wafer so that it stands on its edge on the cup.

(If a woodworker is available, the chalice may be made in wood, which is more durable than foam. The wooden chalice can be finished in the same way as the styrofoam cup.)

While the chalice in the full round is shown, its back may be cut off as shown by the right background pattern on page 24. The cut-off cup may be easier to handle if the star is one-half inch foam. But when the star is thicker, it will accept a fully rounded chalice.

Paint the entire cup with styrofoam glue. After it is dry, smooth a knife blade over its surface while applying pressure to push in any rough places on the foam. Paint the cup with glue again; smooth out the rough surfaces. After another coat of glue, sand off rough surfaces with an emery board. Let the cup dry thoroughly after the next coat of glue.

Cover the cup with metallic gold paint. If desired, apply gold metallic leaf over the surface. If they are wanted, glue pearls and/or metallic gold braid or trim in place. Note: A plain chalice which is carefully made can be as beautiful as a highly ornamented one.

The original bread was a flat pearl about 1¼ inches in diameter. A communion wafer or a circle of fiberglass of the same diameter could also be used. (Pieces of wired transparent sequins-by-the-yard may be glued to the back of the bread like a radiance.) For the half-size chalice, a 20 mm round sequin bangle fits. Glue the bread in place. Then spray the entire chalice and wafer with a clear acrylic finish.

STARS

Cut the full-size six-point star by the colored background pattern on page 24 or the half-size by the pattern on page 56. Make cuts in the top and bottom peaks about one-fourth inch deep for the bowl and foot of the cup in the full round only. After the star is glittered, glue the cup onto it. Run pipe cleaner pieces from the star's back into the cup to support it.

BOOK ON SEVEN-POINT STAR

While this Chrismon was not in the original Liturgical Year Series, it was added in 1961. It balances the Sacraments in a presentation of the Means of Grace.

Materials: Gold foil, sequin material, or gold-backed paper; 3 mm or seed pearls; #30 hair or gold beading wire; gold thread; white glue.

Directions:

Cut about twelve 4 by 2 7/8 inch pieces of gold foil, sequin material, or gold-backed paper for the full-size book; cut 2 1/4 by 1 3/8 inch pieces for the half-size book. Fold the "sheets" in half along the dotted line for the pages of the book. (See the half-size pattern on Figure 60 on this page.) With gold thread, sew the pages together along the fold.

Construct the letters W.G.E.F. by the directions for the letters on page 49. But make the wire extensions from the letters three inches long. Use 3 mm pearls for the full-size book, seed pearls for the half-size.

With a pin, punch holes through the pages for the letter wires. Note the positions of the letters on the background pattern on page 27 for the full-size book and on Figure 60 for the half-size. Push the letter wires through the book. On the back of the book, twist the wires together to hold the letters in place.

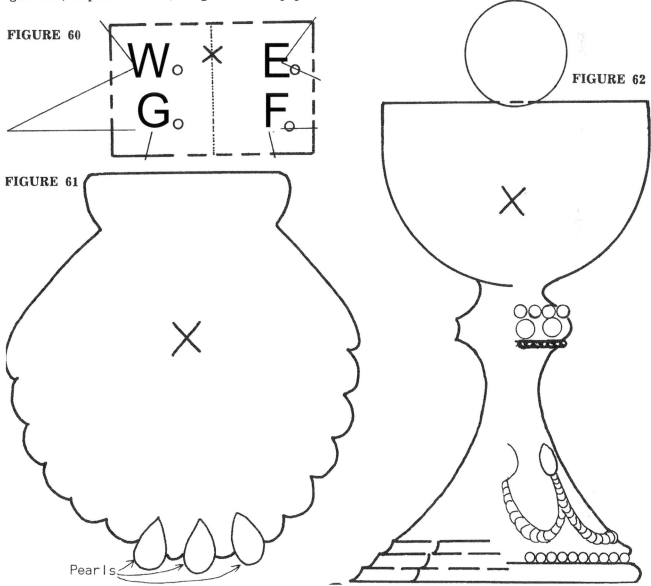

FIGURE 60

FIGURE 61

FIGURE 62

Pearls

57

STARS

Cut out the full-size star by the background pattern on page 27, the half-size by the page 56 pattern. Cut off the star's center front to make a flat surface for the book. After the star is glittered, put glue on its flat face. Position the book on top with the X's coinciding. Run sequin pins through the pearl "dots," the book, and into the star. If necessary, run extra pins through the center fold of the pages.

CROSSES

For the most part, crosses are straight lines and right angles. Since even a child can easily spot irregularities in a straight line, crosses must be made carefully and exactly.

Do not attempt to ornament the crosses of the Christian Year Series beyond the suggestions that are given. For example, if the crosses are made of styrofoam, do not cover the foam with glitter. (But a smooth pearlized finish may be given to the foam.) The shapes of the crosses tell the story. Let their forms show clearly and with a minimum of surface decoration. All efforts should be aimed at doing as smooth and perfect a job as possible.

Because even these full-size crosses are small and light, it is necessary to use three hanging wires to insure that the cross is erect. Generally, one wire should be attached to each horizontal arm. Study each cross and its relationship to the framework to which it is attached to ascertain the best position for the third wire which holds the cross steady in its proper place and plane.

ORIGINAL CROSSES

The original crosses in this Series are made of ivory. Because ivory is an ancient symbol for our Lord's body, ivory crosses are traditional in the church.

Old pianos are the ideal source for this material. Since plastic generally substitutes for piano ivories now, a tuner who repairs or rebuilds pianos is the most likely source of supply.

When piano key ivories are used, the crosses must be pieced from two layers of ivory. The piecing joints must be at different places on the two layers so that a solid piece is under or over each cut. Dotted lines on the full-size Passion Cross on Figure 63 on page 60 show the top layer of ivory while similar lines on the half-size pattern show the cuts in the bottom layer. The points at which these cuts are made must be worked out for each cross individually.

Sometimes the design of the cross makes it advisable to construct it so that its appendages are above or below the surface of the main body of the cross. This situation is illustrated on Figure 63 by the solid lines on some of the half-size crosses. Lines on the Anchor Cross and the Cross Treflée show where the appendages are put on top of the main body of the cross; extra parts of the Cross in Glory and the Fiery Cross are glued under the body of the cross. Attachments on the full size crosses should be handled in the same manner.

If one is sufficiently skillful, ivory joints will not show on the surface of the cross. To hide any clumsiness, use a very small square or triangular file to make shallow grooves at the places shown by the dotted lines on the Cross Crosslet and the Cross of Constantine. Notice that the filing lines, which do not go completely through the top layer, cover any possible junction lines. Work out a similar groove pattern to hide the joints on each cross. Actually, this filing serves to give a simple decoration to the surface of the cross. Beveling the edges of a cross also adds to its appearance.

Make the nine full-size crosses by the colored background patterns on this page, page 4, and the large Passion Cross on Figure 63. The half-size patterns are on Figure 63.

Hangers are clear glass beads cemented at the proper places behind the cross. Glue the beads so that their holes are free. Then run #30 wire through the bead; twist it on itself to hold firmly. The loose ends are the hangers.

* * *

Hints on working ivory: To cut ivory, use a borrowed jeweler's saw. While Duco type cement or white glue may be used, white or clear epoxy cement is more durable. Because water yellows ivory, NEVER use it. To remove surface dirt, wash ivory with alcohol. Ivory yellows with age; sometimes surface yellowing (and slight scratches) can be sanded off with 006 or finer sandpaper. If the ivory is yellowed through, bleach it in the sun. This process takes months of prolonged exposure to strong sunlight.

When the cross is finished, polish it with tripoli (source, Piano repairer) with alcohol as the lubricant. Since ivory is translucent, never use anything dark behind it. Colored beads or even dark glue cast shadows on the surface. Working with this material is tedious and exacting; there is no substitute for patience.

SIMPLIFIED CROSSES

Cut the crosses from one-half inch white styrofoam. Bevel the edges; attach styrofoam hangers as needed. If desired, the styrofoam may be given the smooth finish which is described for the simplified hand on page 37.

* * *

A beautiful substitute for ivory is the vinyl floor tile that looks like marble. This translucent material is available in a white stone-like pattern from most makers of plastic tile. Since the thinner grades can be cut with scissors, it is easy to work. Thicker grades can be cut with X-acto type knives. One nine by nine inch tile is sufficient for the crosses in the Series.

To finish the vinyl crosses, bevel the edges with a very sharp knife. Attach the hanging wires by punching a heavy needle diagonally through the arm so that it runs about one-fourth inch from the edge of the back to the edge of the front. Run a wire through the hole which is made; twist the wire to hold firmly in place. See Figure 64 on page 60.

CROSSES

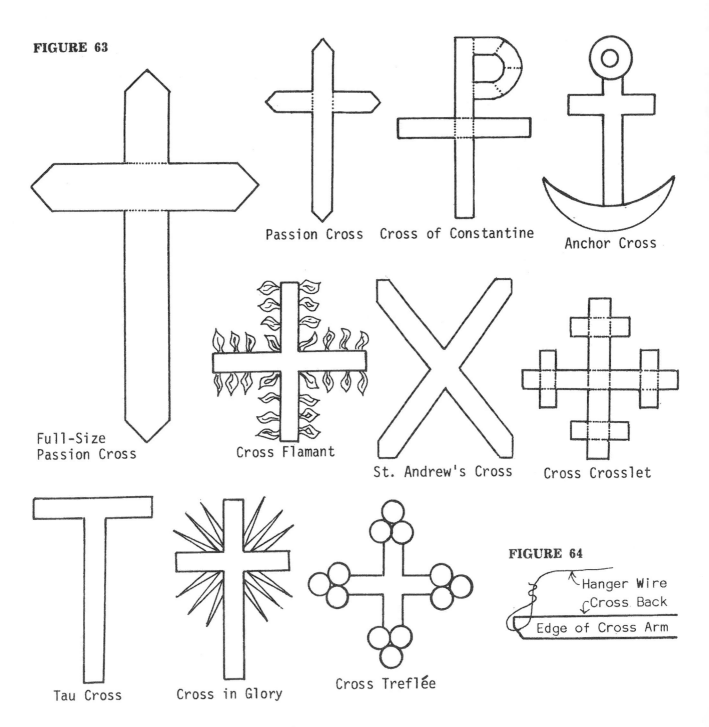

FIGURE 63

Passion Cross | Cross of Constantine | Anchor Cross
Full-Size Passion Cross | Cross Flamant | St. Andrew's Cross | Cross Crosslet
Tau Cross | Cross in Glory | Cross Treflée

FIGURE 64 — Hanger Wire, Cross Back, Edge of Cross Arm

These crosses would look equally well if they were carved from wood. If such a skill is available in a group, let it be used to construct these symbols!

After the crosses are carved, they may be painted white; if desired, add a coat of pearlized spray finish. Or the crosses could be given an antique white finish.

For the hangers, twist pieces of #30 hair wire around small staples in the backs of the crosses.

* * *

At St. Andrew's Church, the Campus Church at Lenoir Rhyne College in Hickory, North Carolina, these crosses were constructed of white milk glass. The horizontal arms were cut in one piece, the vertical members in another. Then they were glued together at the crucial point with epoxy cement. Appendages were glued onto whichever side that they looked best. (Appendages could be of translucent fiberglass.)

St. Andrew's crosses have a lovely translucence; their crisp, refreshing look emphasizes their lines in which the meaning lies.

VINE & TRINITY CYCLE ACCESSORIES

TENDRILS

One of the most characteristic parts of a vine is the curling tendril that appears irregularly. Most of the tendrils on the vines are twisted from the stems of the leaves and bunches of grapes after their stems are run through the holes in the tubing vine. However if it is desired, ten inch pieces of #18 or #20 copper wire may be soldered to the framework to make additional tendrils on the Life cycle.

Form the tendril from the straight wire by wrapping the wire smoothly and evenly around a one-half inch dowel or similar object. Begin to wrap the wire at its point of attachment to the vine (or at the place where it emerges from a hole in the vine). About two inches from the end of the wire, slip the dowel out and substitute a pencil for it. Continue to wrap the wire around the pencil to its point at the end of the wire. Remove the pencil. Pull the curled wire outward to give it length.

LEAVES

All three sizes of leaves shown on Figure 65 below may be mixed for use on the full-size vine although one may prefer to use only the two larger ones. For the half-size vine, use only the smallest size leaf.

Cut the leaves from gold sequin material. Or use two layers of either gold-backed paper or gold foil glued together with the gold sides out. With a stylus, score the main veins (widest lines on the pattern) of the leaf on the top side; score the auxiliary veins (medium width lines on the pattern) on the underside of the leaf. If, in addition to this scoring, the edges of the leaves are rolled slightly with the fingers, the leaf will have a more natural appearance.

The stems of the leaves are pieces (about ten inches long) of 18 or 20 gauge brass wire or copper wire of the same size which is sprayed gold. Bend a tiny circle in one end of the wire.

If the leaves are made of sequin material, the circle and about one inch of stem are stapled and/or taped to the back of the leaf after it is cut out and scored. (Use transparent tape.) But when gold-backed paper or gold (silver-backed) foil are used, that part of the wire which includes the circle and about three inches (two inches in the smallest side) is placed between the pieces of material before they are glued together. When

FIGURE 65

the leaf is cut out, it is positioned so that the wired portion becomes the midrib of the leaf. Finally the leaf is scored.

Attach the leaf to the vine by running the wire through its hole in the framework. Bend the wire that emerges from the framework at a right angle so that it lies next to the tubing for one-fourth inch. Then wire the remainder of the wire around a dowel to form the tendril as explained above.

BUNCHES OF GRAPES

Use stemmed 12 mm to 20 mm gold glass or plastic balls for the grapes. Make the full-size bunches of an assortment of the sizes, the half-size of the smaller balls. If they can be found, use balls with gold stems. When other than gold-stemmed balls must be used, spiral and glue a one-fourth inch wide strip of gold-backed paper around the stem to hide the color.

Twist an end of a piece of #30 wire around a stem to hold close to the ball. Place two more balls about one-half inch above the first ball; wrap the #30 wire around all the stems to hold them together. Add the fourth ball; continue to wrap the #30 wire up the stem.

If the balls which are wired together are to look like grapes, they must be arranged to give that appearance as they are wired; they will not fall into place naturally. Sometimes a cluster of three or four balls which are already wired to each other is added. This helps to build out the bunch at its widest parts.

Only one stem extends from the top of the bunch. Therefore, after the stem of the fourth ball is wired in place, cut the stems off the first three balls close to the #30 wrapping wire. As more balls are added by wrapping their stems, continue to cut off the previously attached stems so that only one or two long stems extend from the bunch.

Atop the bunch, cut off all the leftover stems. With the leftover #30 wire, attach the loop and one inch of the end of a ten inch wire (like the leaf stems) to the top of the wired together stems. (Framework holes allow the entry of only one wire.) Attach the grapes to the framework like the leaves described above.

Exact directions for this job cannot be given. Real bunches of grapes vary in size and shape. Consequently, the fruits here should differ. While the sizes may be similar, give the grapes a naturally varied appearance. Generally 25 to 30 balls make up a full-size bunch; it measures about four to five inches long and is about seven inches in circumference at its fullest. The half-size uses about 14 balls for a bunch about three inches long. Figure 66 on this page illustrates an average full-size bunch of grapes.

* * *

The grapes may also be made from glass or metal gold beads. For such bunches, follow the directions on page 20 in *Chrismons for Every Day*. Use 12 mm to 16 mm beads for the full-size, 8 mm to 12 mm beads for the half-size fruits. Make the finished bunches the sizes listed above.

* * *

If desired, gold polyethylene artificial grapes may be used. Let their sizes correspond to those previously mentioned. Since these artificial bunches do not have a shiny finish, they do not match other Chrismons as they could. But if their dull appearance is not objectionable, by all means use them.

PEARLS

Pearls to symbolize the Word of God were used on the original Liturgical Year Series in 1960. But the addition of the book on the star in 1961 makes the pearls in this grouping somewhat redundant. If they are wanted, however, use them.

Run an eight inch piece of #30 wire through a large pearl about 24 mm or one inch in diameter. Twist the ends of the wire to hold around the pearl. Fasten the pearls onto the Trinity cycle by twisting the leftover #30 wire around the bolts on the framework.

If large pearls cannot be found, center three smaller pearls on the #30 wire. Attach this cluster to the framework as directed tbove.

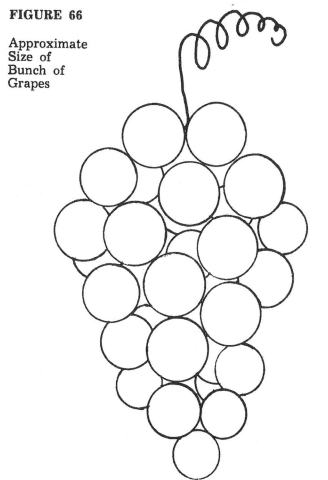

FIGURE 66

Approximate Size of Bunch of Grapes

ACCESSORIES

CENSERS

Photographs: Original, page 65; Present, page 22.

ORIGINAL CENSERS:

The base of the original censer is a one inch gold Christmas tree ball. Remove the metal top and the hanger wire from the ball. Pinch the loop of wire together at point A on Figure 67 below. Place a half inch ornamental gold sequin, B, over both ends of the wire. Push the wire ends into the ball to hold the sequin over the ball's hole, which is the bottom of the censer.

The harness which fits over the censer and by which it is hung is made of gold rocailles on beading wire. First, string enough beads on the wire to make a circle, C, around the neck of the ball. The ends of the C circle wire become two (D and E) of the censer's three hanging wires. Make hanger F by twisting another length of wire on the circle wire so that wires D, E, and F are equally spaced around the circle.

String beads on each wire to circle G. Make circle G like circle C, but fit the circle to its diagramed place on the ball. String beads on wires D and E from both circles C and G to circle H; loop wire F around circle G's wire; string beads on F to circle H. Make circle H and join it to the harness as G was added. Continue to string beads on each set of D, E, and F wires to the joining point J.

Cut off the extra D and E wires from circles G and H. Run the remaining D, E, and F wires through one bead; straight-line anchor the bead in place. The leftover wire becomes the hanger.

Make circle K the same size as C. Continue the wires until each bead carries two wires. Twist the wires together. Lay W, strands of glass wool (Cloud on page 37), over the circle. Bend the twisted wires to hold the wool in place; cut off the excess wires. Glue K and the wool at the middle of K to the top of the ball.

PRESENT CENSER:

The bowl of this censer is the stem half of a one inch or 24 mm gold stemmed plastic ball. Remove the stem to expose the ball's hole.

Make a straight weave, A on Figure 68 below, of gold rocailles on beading wire to exactly fit around the top edge of the bowl. Backweave to anchor the wires. Make another straight weave, B, on the top edge of weave A. The top edge lengthwise beads of circle A become the outer lengthwise beads of the second circle B. B's crossover and inner lengthwise beads are bent toward the inside of the bowl to form a lip over the top edge of the bowl. See Detail 1.

Shape a 16 mm gold filigree cup finding, C, around the outside of the base of the bowl. Loop a length of beading wire around a line at the edge of the filigree. Run rocailles over both wire ends; push the beads tight against the filigree. String the beads from C to A. Weave the D wires up through the A weave. Continue to string beads on D up to the joining point J. In like manner, attach hangers E and F to C, string the beads, weave through A, and bead the wires to J. Position D, E, and F so that they are equally spaced around the C and A circles.

At J, cut one wire off each D, E, and F hanger. Run a 5 mm gold bead J over the remaining D, E, and F wires. Straight-line anchor the wires. The leftover wire is the hanger.

Center a rocaille on a length of beading wire. Run both ends of the wire through K (a 5 mm gold bead), the center of C, and the hole in the bottom of the bowl. String two 5 mm gold beads on each wire end. Pull the wires tight, twist them together, and cut off their excess.

Put some glue in the bottom of the bowl. Push the ends of pieces of glass wool (Cloud on page 37) into the glue to simulate smoke from the censer. Let the glue dry thoroughly.

FIGURE 67

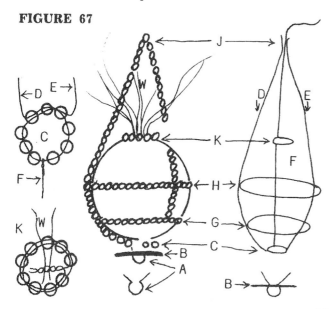

FIGURE 68

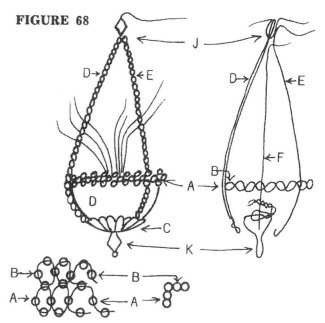

OTHER CHRISMON BOOKS AVAILABLE

CHRISMONS: BASIC SERIES

This book contains material basic to the construction and use of all the Chrismons regardless of the Series in which they appear. General information, covered only in the *Basic Series*, includes: The history, purpose, and meaning of the Chrismons and the Chrismon tree; general construction procedures and methods; ways to adapt patterns and construction methods; materials and supplies and their sources; and a general interpretation of all the Chrismons. To use either the *Christian Year, Every Day*, or the *Advanced Series*, one should have the *Basic Series* as a guide and reference.

The *Basic Series* gives patterns, diagrams, and step-by-step directions for thirty Chrismons as well as a complete explanation of the meaning of each. For some of the patterns, several variations are shown. Designs include monograms of and symbols for our Lord and God. In general, Chrismons in the *Basic Series* are easier to construct than those in the other three books. About one-third of the patterns are suitable in size for either home or church trees. Home-size as well as the original church-size patterns are given for half of the remaining ornaments. A Christmas program or pageant that explains Chrismons in the *Basic Series* is included.

The instructions for the *Basic Series* were revised and reprinted during the summer of 1972. The printing includes photographs of all the Chrismons in the Series.

CHRISMONS FOR EVERY DAY

This most recent of the Chrismon books was released in the autumn of 1971. It is recommended for beginners, intermediate, and advanced Chrismon workers. Beginners will find it a valuable supplement to the *Basic Series* because *Chrismons for Every Day* offers new construction methods for learners and complete and specific workshop guides and outlines. Intermediate and advanced workers as well as beginners will find detailed directions and patterns for miniatures in this book. In addition, any Chrismon maker will be interested in the more than thirty new patterns for medium and large tree decorations. There are crosses, monograms, and symbols — all combined in different ways — as well as a set of eight Chrismons, the Beatitudes. Ornaments vary from very easy to difficult to make.

The main focus of *Chrismons for Every Day*, however, is on demonstrating inspirational uses for these Christian symbols throughout the year. Among the pictured suggestions for which patterns and directions are given are hangings, arrangements, mobiles, pictures, shadowboxes, wedding cake toppers, wreaths, and bookmarks.

As with all the Chrismon books, complete interpretations for all the designs in this book are given. Since these Chrismons were developed a few years after the last previous book, new materials and finishes which hobbyists will enjoy using make up some of the new designs. A number of the pictures of the finished Chrismons are in color.

CHRISMONS: ADVANCED SERIES

This Series is composed of both individual Chrismons (as in the Basic book) and groups or sets of Chrismons. While the individual ornaments in these sets are related to each other in meaning and are somewhat similar in design, they are not physically connected as are the Chrismons of the Christian Year Series. The whole set need not be constructed or used. Two of the several groups included are the "Angels and Archangels" and the "Parable Balls." Some of the single Chrismons are the "Crown of Thorns," "Wheat and Grapes," "Palms," and various crosses not in either of the other Series.

Only one size pattern is given in this Series. Over half the Chrismons in it, however, are suitable for either home or church use. The designs range from easy to very difficult to make. The worship program in the *Advanced Series* makes use of Chrismons from the *Basic, Christian Year*, and *Advanced Series*. By only a slight change, the *Christian Year Series* group can be omitted.

The instructions for the *Advanced Series* were revised and reprinted during the spring of 1973. The printing includes photographs, some in color, of all the Chrismons in the Series.

No Chrismon designs or patterns are duplicated in any of the Series.

CHRISMONS FOR CHILDREN

Many of you have asked over the years about something for the children relating to the Chrismons Tree. We are happy to announce the publishing of a children's storybook, in color, **Samuel Sparrow and The Tree of Light.** This is wonderful story and a must for all children. This is a perfect gift for that special child in your life. (23pgs.) 8 1/2 x 6 1/2 ISBN # 0-9715472-5-4 - Library of Congress # 2003107199

CHRISMONS

The book which is simply titled *Chrismons* contains condensed interpretations of all the ornaments on the tree at The Lutheran Church of the Ascension in Danville, Virginia. A full color photograph of the tree is on the cover while drawings and photographs of some of the Chrismons illustrate the explanations. The book is arranged in such a way that it is also a handy reference on Christian symbolism.

Made in United States
Orlando, FL
27 August 2022